RONDA K. SALAZAR

# Roar Like A Woman

*35 Empowering Words To Unleash Your Inner Lioness*

# Contents

## III Rise Up

## IV Lead with Vision

## V Awaken Curiosity

# Before You Begin

This book is based on the author's personal experiences, opinions, and reflections. This content is intended for educational and motivational purposes only and should not be considered professional advice.

Readers are encouraged to consult qualified professionals for guidance in areas such as mental health, medical issues, legal matters, or financial decisions.

The author and publisher disclaim any liability for any outcomes resulting from the use of the information contained in this book. This is your journey, and no one else can walk it for you—so please take what resonates, and leave the rest.

As the author, I want to add this personally: I care deeply about your well-being. If you or someone you love is struggling with emotional distress or mental health challenges, please know you're not alone. A list of national crisis resources is included at the back of this book in the section titled *You Are Not Alone*. These organizations offer free, confidential support—many of which are available 24 hours a day, 7 days a week.

*You don't find your roar. You remember it.*
—Ronda K. Salazar

# Dedication

**For my parents—**

You raised me to be strong, kind, and unstoppable. Through your faith and never-ending compassion, you created a safe space for so many, allowing them to find their footing in a world that had let them down.

Your examples of empathy and quiet strength are the foundations of who I am today. Your love lives on in every word I write.

*And your legacy lives on in the roar I now carry forward.*

# Acknowledgments

**To my big brother, Ron—**
Thank you for teaching me to read before I even started school, for keeping me entertained with creativity and humor (even when you were just trying to keep me out of your hair!), and for being my rock during some of the hardest moments of my life.

I could always count on you. And I still can. I love you.

**To my Bugaboo—**
May you always know your worth, speak your truth, and chase joy without apology.

If this book teaches you anything, let it be this:
    Your voice matters.
    Your fire matters.
    You matter.

I'm forever proud to be your mom.

**To Howard—my best friend and fiercest cheerleader.**
I am forever grateful for the years we shared together. Your unwavering belief in me helped me believe in myself.

I know you'll continue to rise, grow, and thrive in pursuit of your own dreams. Keep shining and being larger than life.

**To Jay Marzette—**

In a world that never stops evolving, you remind me that mentorship is a two-way street.

Thank you for your insight, encouragement, and for helping me grow in ways I never expected.

**To the many friends I've had the honor of working with throughout my career—**

You've helped shape who I am today, through every experience, every project, every challenge, and every conversation.

Thank you for always believing in me, even when I didn't believe in myself yet.

**And to every woman—and every ally—holding this book—**

Thank you for trusting me with your time and letting me share parts of my life with you.

I hope this helps you remember your roar.

**With gratitude,**
*Ronda*

# Introduction

Like many of you, I have spent most of my adult life in the corporate world—trying to climb the corporate ladder, learning to read between the lines and adjust to unspoken dynamics, and juggling side hustles to feed my creative and entrepreneurial spirit. While much of what I share in the pages that follow is shaped by my perspective as a leader in business spaces, the lessons in this book extend far beyond the boardroom. These words apply to life, love, resilience, and self-worth—across every stage, every setting, and every season of your life.

I operated by the book for years—playing it safe, staying in my lane, and letting expectations guide my path. But eventually, something inside me began to stir. I began to question whether success was really about job titles, performance reviews, and perfectly executed PowerPoint presentations. I began to crave something more meaningful, more personal—something that aligned with my core being.

That stirring led me on a journey of reflection, growth, and self-discovery. I began journaling regularly. I wrote music. I got quiet enough to hear the voice inside me that had been whispering all along. And when I finally listened, I heard my inner lioness roar. She reminded me that I wasn't meant to shrink myself to fit anyone's mold. I was meant to lead, create, inspire, and empower—not just myself but others, too.

This book was born from that transformation and my personal journey.

*Roar Like A Woman* is not just a collection of words. It is more than just stories and advice. It is a movement—a call to action for women everywhere to step into their full, unshakable power and to own their voice and their worth. Together, we rise. We lift each other. We amplify the parts of ourselves that have been silenced, shamed, or overlooked. And in doing so, we awaken a version of ourselves that is fierce, whole, and fully alive.

You will encounter 35 words in this book—each word carefully chosen for its role in helping you unlock the most empowered, confident, purpose-filled version of yourself. These are not just words—they are mantras, affirmations, and sparks intended to ignite a fire within you.

The book is divided into five parts, each designed to guide you through a different phase of personal empowerment:

- **Part I: Rooted in Self** – Explore identity, worth, and inner truth
- **Part II: Ignite the Spark** – Reconnect with energy, joy, and passion
- **Part III: Rise Up** – Embrace resilience, strength, and courageous action
- **Part IV: Lead with Vision** – Step into purpose, power, and impact
- **Part V: Awaken Curiosity** – Cultivate growth, creativity, and lifelong discovery

Each chapter is a short, powerful reflection anchored by a word that embodies a particular aspect of empowerment. Some words will feel like old friends— comfortable, familiar, and affirming. Others might challenge you. They may push you to confront parts of yourself that you've kept hidden or neglected. And that's okay. Growth requires discomfort. And evolution requires courage.

What sets this book apart is that it blends personal storytelling with practical skill-building. Each chapter begins with a reflection on the empowerment word—how I've lived it, learned from it, or struggled with it. Then, you'll find a section inviting you to take an honest look at whether you're holding yourself back from fully embracing the power of that word. This reflection section is meant to gently challenge the internalized stories and limiting beliefs we've absorbed over time. Through key questions and insights, you'll be invited to examine how you might be standing in your own way—and begin releasing what no longer serves you.

Finally, I'll share actionable strategies and mindset shifts that can help you strengthen your connection to that word in your life.

This isn't a textbook on how to be empowered. It's something more personal—and more honest.

*This is a memoir in motion,*
*a reflection of how I've tried*
*to live, stumble, rise, and grow*
*into each of these words myself.*

I'm not here to preach from a pedestal—I'm walking this path right alongside you. My hope is that in sharing my story, you'll feel braver sharing yours. That you'll start to recognize your own strength in the messy, beautiful, ordinary moments of life. That, together, we'll rise.

As you move through these pages, my intention is that you'll start to see yourself more clearly—and more lovingly. That you'll begin to rewrite the narrative in your head and believe, with conviction, that *you are worthy, beautiful, powerful, and whole—exactly as you are.*

Although this book was written by a woman and for women, its lessons and stories are universal. If you're a man reading this—whether you're here to grow, understand the women in your life better, or support someone you love—know that you are welcome here. Empowerment isn't gendered. It's human. And your roar matters, too.

This book is for everyone:

- The woman who's leading teams and driving strategy from the board-room.
- The recent graduate stepping nervously into her first big role.
- The stay-at-home mom who wants to rediscover her voice and claim space outside of her caregiving identity.
- The survivor who's rebuilding from loss or trauma.
- The quiet one who's ready to speak up.
- The bold one who needs a reminder that softness is strength, too.

*Whoever you are, wherever you are on your journey,*
*this book is for you.*

It's my deepest wish that you come to the end of these chapters not only feeling inspired but equipped with tools to help you fully step into the empowered lioness that already exists within you. I want you to walk away with a renewed sense of self, a deeper appreciation for your story, and the fierce, unshakable knowledge that your roar matters.

Let this book be your permission slip. Your invitation to rise. Your reminder that you were never meant to play small. Let's go on this journey together.

Let's roar like women.

# I

# Rooted in Self

# Identity and Inner Worth

*Before you can rise, roar, or lead, you must know*
*who you are—and believe, without hesitation,*
*that you are enough.*

This part of the self-discovery journey starts with your roots: your self-identity and your inner worth. These are not things the world hands you. They are truths you claim, embody, and protect—even when the world tries to convince you otherwise.

If you've ever questioned your value, doubted your beauty, or silenced your voice to avoid being "too much," you're not alone. Every woman has felt that tension between who she is and who she thinks she should be.

And much of that tension is rooted in bias—deeply ingrained and often unspoken. We've been shaped by messages from childhood, by cultural expectations, and by the double standards that still persist in society today. A man who asserts himself is seen as confident; a woman who does the same is often labeled as aggressive or emotional. These quiet, persistent biases shape not just how others see us, but how we see ourselves. Until we begin to recognize and challenge them—boldly and holistically—we will continue to be diminished by them. For women, especially in professional spaces, this often means being expected to feel less, ask less, expect less, and take up less space.

*But I'm not here to take up less space.*
*And neither are you.*

3

Here's what I want you to remember: You don't need to become someone else to be powerful. You simply need to reconnect with who you already are.

The themes explored in Part I—like *Confident, Authentic, Worthy, Unique,* and *Refined*—will guide you inward as you reconnect with identity, worth, and truth. They'll challenge you to peel back old stories, reclaim your truth, and begin seeing yourself not through the eyes of judgment, but through the lens of wholeness.

As you read, reflect, and apply each word, I invite you to do something radical: *stop apologizing for existing.* Start celebrating how you think, speak, feel, and show up in the world. The following chapters are not just about feeling better—they're about knowing better and knowing that you are already whole. Already powerful. Already more than enough.

So let's begin where all strength is born: from within.

**You are not missing anything.**
**You are rediscovering everything.**

# Beautiful

## What It Means to Be Beautiful

The word beautiful traces back to the Latin root *bellus*, meaning "pretty, charming, fine." But somewhere along the way, that meaning got hijacked by glossy magazines, filtered selfies, and society's narrow standards—and beautiful started to feel like a word that didn't belong to me. It felt like a word reserved for someone else—someone airbrushed, someone perfect, someone I wasn't.

This word has always been a struggle for me to embrace. Our culture is saturated with images—billboards, social media, commercials—all curated to portray beauty as something flawless, exclusive, and often unattainable. And let's be honest: those images aren't representative of the vibrant diversity of the world we actually live in. The standard has been set by a mirage—something polished, posed, and often digitally enhanced. And when you don't see yourself reflected in those standards, you start to question your worth.

As a teen, and even into my twenties, I battled with what it meant to *be beautiful*. I wasn't the girl turning heads in the hallways. I wasn't the one pursued by every guy in school. I didn't feel like I was the kind of girl people wrote songs about or stopped in their tracks for. And for a long time, I believed that made me less. Less desirable. Less seen. Less valuable. Less.

I recall a particularly painful moment from high school that has etched itself into my memory. I wasn't in the popular crowd but had a close-knit group of friends—Donna, Cathy, Kevin, and me. We were like the four Musketeers, always hanging out together. I quietly had a crush on Kevin—not because he was particularly dreamy, but because he had a bit of a rebel streak and always made me laugh.

One spring, Kevin asked me to the prom. I was thrilled, and, of course, I said "yes." My mom made my prom dress, a beautiful rose-pink color, and we dyed satin shoes and gloves to match. But then, a week before prom, Kevin told me he wasn't going anymore. He said he had changed his mind—that it was just a silly dance and he didn't feel like participating. I was blindsided and heartbroken. I had been so excited—it was my first prom, and I didn't want to miss out on the experience.

My mom saved the day by suggesting I ask Kurt, a friend from church, to escort me. The only problem? Kevin had just demolished my self-confidence, leaving me completely unsure of myself.

I didn't feel beautiful. I didn't even feel visible. I had been dumped just days before prom, and the wound was still fresh. I remember standing in front of the phone, heart racing, rehearsing what I'd say. It felt like I was asking for pity—not a date.

"Would you... maybe, possibly... go with me? Just as friends?"

Every version I came up with made me feel smaller, as if I were asking for something I didn't deserve. But somewhere in all that fear and self-doubt, I found the courage to make the call.

And he said "yes!" For the next few days at school, I did my best to avoid Kevin, but I made sure Donna and Cathy both knew I wasn't going alone. I had a date!

When prom night came, Kurt and I showed up together—me in my rose-pink dress, hand-made with love by my mother, and Kurt with a matching rose-pink tie. Just before I walked out the door, I remember my mom leaning in and whispering, "Kevin doesn't know what he's missing."

I don't remember her exact words, but I remember how they made me feel—like I was worth showing up for. Like I didn't need anyone's permission to feel beautiful that night.

And guess who was already out on the dance floor when we walked in?

Kevin.

Dancing with my best friend—Donna.

They hadn't told me. I was crushed. And of course, I didn't just feel betrayed—I felt like it was about me. That I wasn't pretty enough.

Donna had a short, sassy haircut and a fashion sense that turned heads. She carried herself with an ease and confidence I couldn't fake. By comparison, I felt invisible.

That moment didn't just break my heart—it **broke something deeper**.

It cemented a belief I carried for years:

*Beauty was something I lacked.*

*Beauty was something other girls had.*

*Beauty was something that could be taken from me—without warning, without explanation, without apology.*

It would take decades before I questioned that belief—and even longer before I rewrote it.

My parents would always tell me, "Beauty comes from within." But to a young girl surrounded by the messaging of magazines and movies, those words felt like a consolation, like a kind way of saying, "You're not traditionally pretty, but that's okay." I didn't truly understand what "Beauty comes from within" meant until adulthood. It took time. Life. Experience. And a complete redefinition of the word for myself.

Now, I know. Beauty does live on the inside. It radiates from your very soul. It lives in your warmth, your optimism, your empathy, and your light. It's in the way you show up for others, in the way you carry yourself, and in the energy you bring into every room you enter.

Today, I know I'm beautiful—not just in appearance, but in spirit. I am a woman in her 50s, and I often get compliments stating that I look 10 to 12 years younger than I am. Want to know my secret? It's not skincare. It's not makeup. It's not good lighting. It's this: *I've embraced the truth that real beauty starts within.* That radiance shows when you nurture your spirit, love who you are, and live with joy and compassion. You glow. You shine. Inner beauty is magnetic—it becomes outer beauty.

I've learned that my inner beauty is reflected in the way I love people deeply, in the way I lead with positivity, and in the kindness and empathy I extend to others. My beauty is revealed in my laughter, curiosity, resilience, and passion. It's all of the things that make me *me.*

So when someone tells me I'm beautiful now, I believe them. And I smile—not because I finally fit someone's definition, but because I've created my own. I own my beauty. And I want that for you, too.

## Are You Holding Yourself Back?

Have you internalized someone else's definition of beauty?

Maybe you've found yourself comparing your body, hair, skin, and even your smile, to what you see on social media. Perhaps you've stood in front of the mirror picking apart the very features that make you unique. Maybe, like me, you once thought you weren't "beautiful enough" to be seen, heard, loved, or celebrated.

It's easy to fall into the trap of believing beauty must be chased, earned, or manufactured.

But the real prison is in believing you're not enough as you are.

*Our minds are powerful storytellers,*
*and if we keep repeating the lie that we're not beautiful,*
*we begin to live like it's true.*

Let's challenge that. Ask yourself:

- Do I criticize myself more than I compliment myself?
- Do I seek validation through appearance instead of aligning with who I truly am?
- Do I believe beauty is limited to youth, size, or perfection?
- Have I ever dimmed my light because I didn't feel attractive enough to shine?

These are hard questions, but important ones.

*We can't reclaim our beauty*
*if we don't first recognize where we've given it away.*
*And why.*

If any of these resonate, it might be time to unlearn society's version of beauty—and rediscover your own. The truth is, beauty is not a look. It's a feeling. It's an energy. It's a state of being. And you are allowed—invited, even—to redefine it for yourself.

## Building the Skill: How to Step into Your Beauty

Yes, beauty is a skill. Not the kind you master with a makeup tutorial—but one you develop by tuning into your essence and learning to love what already exists within you.

Here's how to start:

1. **Redefine the word.**
   Write down your personal definition of beauty. Be intentional. Think beyond appearances. Consider qualities like kindness, strength, authenticity, and joy. What makes someone truly beautiful to you? Chances are, it's not airbrushed skin or perfect symmetry—it's laughter, warmth, courage, and light. Then, claim those qualities in yourself. Let your definition become your truth.
2. **Compliment yourself daily.**
   Most of us are our own worst critics. Flip the script. Every morning, look yourself in the mirror and affirm something beautiful about who you are: *I am radiant. My energy is magnetic. My presence lights up the room.* At first, it might feel awkward. Say it anyway. Say it loud and say it proud. The more you speak it, the more you'll believe it—and the more it becomes real.
3. **Curate your environment.**
   What we consume affects how we feel. If your media feed is full of unrealistic beauty ideals, it's time to unfollow and refresh. Fill your

life with voices that reflect genuine, raw, diverse beauty—people who inspire, uplift, and empower. Surround yourself with those who not only see your beauty but remind you of it often.

4. **Glow from the inside.**

True beauty starts in your habits. Prioritize emotional well-being. Eat foods that nourish you. Move your body with love. Laugh often. Sleep well. Spend time with people who make your soul feel safe and seen. When you treat your body and spirit with care, you naturally become more vibrant, more grounded, more *you*.

5. **Share your shine.**

Let your beauty be a gift to the world. Smile at strangers. Speak with kindness. Extend empathy. Lift others up. The light that radiates from within you is more beautiful than anything cosmetic on the outside. Beauty isn't selfish—it's irresistible. And when you share it? It becomes contagious.

6. **Celebrate aging.**

We live in a culture obsessed with youth, but aging is not the enemy—it's a privilege. Every line on your face tells a story, and every gray hair is a reminder of wisdom. Let yourself grow older with grace, pride, and power. Beauty doesn't fade—it evolves, and often, it deepens.

7. **Be fully, unapologetically you.**

The most beautiful people are those who own who they are without shame. When you stop apologizing for your quirks, your size, your voice, your shine—you become magnetic. You become unforgettable. You become the definition of beauty.

It took me well into adulthood to realize that beauty is so much more than skin deep. When you learn to love and embrace the inner qualities that make you uniquely you, your outer beauty begins to reflect that empowered spirit—and the glow becomes undeniable.

## Final Roar

Beauty isn't something you chase. It's something you embrace. It begins deep within your soul and flows outward through your words, your energy, and your presence. The moment you stop trying to *look* beautiful and start choosing to *be* beautiful, in how you treat yourself and others, you become radiant in a way that no filter could ever capture.

> *You are already beautiful.*
> *Not because of how you appear,*
> *but because of who you are.*

Let that truth shine.

# Confident

## What It Means to Be Confident

I didn't always think of myself as confident. There were times when I faked it so convincingly that even I believed the act. But here's what I've learned: confidence isn't a personality trait—it's a choice. A skill. A practice.

The word confident comes from the Latin *confidentia*, meaning "firmly trusting, full of trust". It's not about arrogance. It's about assurance. Quiet strength. It doesn't shout. It simply *knows*.

A confident woman is grounded in her own identity. She's secure in her skills, aware of her worth, and not easily shaken by the opinions of others. Confidence is a reflection of self-awareness, not self-importance.

Still, even the most self-aware among us aren't immune to doubt. I've got a voice in my head I like to call the Self-Confidence Devil. She's small, sly, and surprisingly loud for her size. She shows up at the worst moments— whenever I'm about to take a risk, speak boldly, or challenge a norm. And trust me, she's had years of practice.

I recall one of my first corporate presentations, early in my career. I was part of a project team, and we had to present our work to senior government officials. I had done the research, prepared the materials, and knew the content. But the moment I stood up, that familiar voice started in.

"You're too inexperienced. You're going to mess this up. They're not going to take you seriously."

My hands trembled. My voice cracked. But I kept going.

And then—two senior male colleagues, both highly respected, did something subtle but powerful. One gave me a calm, steady nod that grounded me in the moment. The other gently supported one of my answers when I stumbled—not to correct, but to clarify. They didn't speak over me. They didn't take the spotlight. They simply created space for me to rise.

That was the moment I realized: confidence isn't something you wait to feel. It's something you build through action, vulnerability, and repetition.

And sometimes? You borrow a little belief from others until your own kicks in.

So, are you a confident person? Have you ever paused to really try it on for size?

Let's do it together. Read this out loud:

### I am confident.

Three small words. Monumental power. Say it again. Louder this time.

### I. Am. Confident.

One more time—this time, mean it with every fiber of your being.

### I! Am! Confident!

Did you feel it? That internal shift, that little surge of power rising up inside you? That's the energy we're tapping into!

Here's the thing: sometimes, you have to fake it until you make it. That's not a lie—it's a strategy. It's a common approach in the journey of building confidence. When you don't *feel* confident, you can still *act* confident. And over time, the feeling catches up.

Notice that word—*feel*. A simple four-letter word, and yet it can be a woman's greatest hurdle. Why? For generations, women have been labeled "too emotional"—told that passion or raised voices make us unstable or dramatic. That bias shows up everywhere—from the boardroom to the dinner table.

When a man speaks with conviction, he's applauded as strong and assured. When a woman does the same, she risks being labeled emotional or aggressive. Why do our voices still have to push harder just to be heard at the same volume?

Let's get real: this isn't just about perception—it's about programming.

Many people carry deep-rooted biases shaped by the women who raised them. And those biases often go unchallenged—especially when we aren't encouraged to examine how we view women in leadership roles. When a female leader shows compassion, she is instantly categorized into a nurturing role—projected as the mother, the caregiver, the one who feels. And while there is nothing wrong with being nurturing, it doesn't mean we lack logic or leadership. We are not limited by our kindness. We are not defined by our compassion. We can be both nurturing *and* bold.

And yet, that unconscious bias still lurks. The moment we challenge an idea or speak with authority, that little bias monster rears its head and whispers, "too emotional." It's a dilemma that women are all too familiar with.

So, how do we break it?

*We call it out.*
*We own our power.*
*And we show up anyway.*

Because here's the truth: confidence doesn't require permission. It doesn't ask for validation. It is built—through choices, actions, and sometimes, through defiance.

Every once in a while, before I speak up or walk into a meeting, she shows up—that Self-Confidence Devil, with her well-known voice whispering, "Who do you think you are?" She's good. She's sneaky. And she's been with me longer than I care to admit. But I've learned to recognize her tricks. She thrives on hesitation. She feeds on fear. And the best way to defeat her is to drown her out with boldness.

## Are You Holding Yourself Back?

Lack of confidence is a silent saboteur. It creeps into your thoughts, your words, your body language—until one day you realize you've been dimming your light just to make others more comfortable.

Ask yourself this:

- Have you ever walked into a conversation full of knowledge, only to second-guess yourself into silence?
- Have you ever lost control of a meeting or discussion because you were too unsure to speak with authority?
- Have you ever let someone else's louder voice override your truth?

I've been there—more than once. I've sat in rooms where I knew I had the answer—but let my inner Self-Confidence Devil whisper, "You're not good enough. You're not smart enough." And when I let her win, the conversation often derails. Confidence isn't just about feeling bold—it's about reclaiming control.

When we don't believe in our own value, we miss opportunities. We stay quiet when we should speak up. We accept less than we deserve. We shrink when we should rise. And often, we watch others—less qualified, but louder—walk away with the promotion, the credit, the spotlight.

Let's be honest. We've all seen someone who fills the room with bravado—talking over others, inflating their own accomplishments, performing confidence like it's a one-person show. And more often than not, that performance gets mistaken for genuine skill. It's frustrating—but also revealing.

Here's the radical idea: if they're allowed to fake it, so are we. Use your fake confidence like a launchpad—not a mask. Speak the words. Walk the walk until your truth catches up with your energy.

Confidence is a muscle. And just like any other muscle, it needs practice, repetition, and *belief.* So if your confidence is running low, don't worry. You're not broken—you're just untrained. And that's fixable.

## Building the Skill: How to Practice Confidence

So, how do you build confidence when it feels out of reach? How do you silence the Self-Confidence Devil and step fully into your power? It starts with practice—small, intentional steps taken day after day. The good news? Confidence is a skill, and that means it can be learned, strengthened, and mastered.

Confidence isn't something you're born with—it's something you build. And like any worthwhile trait, it takes intentional practice. Here are some strategies to help you strengthen your confidence and quiet your inner Self-Confidence Devil:

1. **Speak the mantra.**
   Say it with power: *I. Am. Confident.* Repeat this daily—in the mirror, in the car, wherever you need a boost. Saying it out loud trains your brain to align your inner belief with your outer voice.

2. **Use affirmations that reflect your strength.**
   Write and recite 3–5 affirmations that reinforce your power and presence. Try statements like: *I trust my voice and my perspective. I bring value into every room I enter. I am capable, competent, and worthy.* Post them where you'll see them daily—on your mirror, phone background, or planner.

3. **Replace comparison with gratitude.**
   Comparison steals confidence. Gratitude restores it. List three things you're proud of or grateful for each day about yourself. It can be a trait, an accomplishment, or how you showed up that day.

4. **Turn weaknesses into growth projects.**
   Instead of hiding from areas you want to improve, tackle them head-on. Choose one thing—like conflict resolution, public speaking, or boundary-setting—and commit to learning more about it. And remember to *ROAR* your way through it: **Read, Observe, Act, Reflect**. It's a simple cycle that turns awareness into progress—and progress builds confidence.

5. **Track your wins.**

   Create a confidence journal. Record every time you speak up, set a boundary, take a risk, or succeed. Even small wins matter. Over time, you'll build a record of proof that you are strong and capable.

6. **Channel your inner lioness.**

   You can be both compassionate and powerful. Speak with clarity and calm. Stand tall. Hold eye contact. Let your body language reflect the inner assurance you are cultivating. Power and kindness are not mutually exclusive.

7. **Take action before you feel "ready".**

   Confidence grows in motion. Don't wait to feel 100% ready—you'll never take the leap. Start now. Speak up now. Raise your hand, send the email, schedule the conversation. Each bold step makes the next one easier.

## Final Roar

*You are no less capable than anyone else.*
*You are not behind.*
*You are not "too emotional."*
*You are powerful.*
*You are wise.*
*You are more than enough.*

And if you ever forget that, remember this: *I. Am. Confident.*

Say it again. Say it louder. Say it until the Self-Confidence Devil, heels clicking and tail tucked, packs up her bags and storms out of your mental space for good.

Because confidence isn't arrogance, it isn't perfection. It's simply the belief that you belong—and the boldness to act like it.

And you *do* belong. So start *believing* it.

# Grace

## What It Means to Lead and Live with Grace

When I think of the word grace, I picture a gentle breeze on a warm day—a quiet strength, a kindness that moves softly but powerfully through us. Grace, in both leadership and life, is not about perfection or ease—it's about presence, compassion, and the ability to make space for humanity, in others and ourselves.

In leadership, grace shows up in how we mentor others, how we guide instead of command, and how we support people through their mistakes as well as their victories. It's the decision to lead with fairness, empathy, and compassion, not fear or rigidity. For instance, when a team member makes a mistake, instead of reprimanding them, a graceful leader would use it as a learning opportunity, guiding them on how to avoid similar errors in the future. True grace allows others to grow in the space we create for them, knowing that mistakes are not just inevitable—they're essential. A great leader doesn't just praise success; they stand behind their people when things go awry, helping them course-correct and try again.

But perhaps the most difficult, and most important, place to practice grace is with ourselves.

This lesson has been one of my most significant personal challenges. I am incredibly hard on myself. No one could ever judge me more harshly than I sometimes judge myself. I set impossibly high expectations—at work, at home, in every area of my life. And when I don't meet those expectations, the inner voice that follows isn't gentle. It doesn't offer support. It chastises. It berates. It tells me I've failed, that I should have done better.

One of the longest-standing examples of this struggle has been my health and weight journey. Early in my career, I worked on an intense year-long project that required 12–16 hour days, seven days a week. I had an expense account for meals, which meant I had free rein at restaurants and zero boundaries. Stress, exhaustion, and poor habits led to a 35-pound weight gain—weight that stayed with me long after the project ended. Over time, the numbers on the scale continued to climb, and eventually, I reached 230 pounds. I was exhausted and discouraged and didn't recognize the woman in the mirror. Most of all, I didn't like what I saw in the mirror—*and I definitely didn't love* the reflection that stared back at me.

Instead of showing myself grace, I punished myself. I threw myself into yo-yo diets, extreme workouts, and cycles of shame and disappointment. I treated every misstep as a failure. It wasn't just about weight—it was about worth. And I was quietly eroding my self-confidence, one failed diet at a time.

Things shifted when I started working with Andrew Dawson, the founder of Royalty Performance and my longtime personal trainer in St. Louis. With his guidance, I lost 30–35 pounds, but more importantly, I began to reframe my perspective on progress and success. Andrew helped me understand that grace is not optional—it is required. That small steps matter. That as long as I am doing my best, I am moving forward. And even when I fall short, it doesn't mean I have failed. (Andrew would probably cringe if he heard me use the word failure at all.)

Grace, he taught me, is what keeps us going. It's the voice that says, Try again. You're still on the path. You're still worthy of love, especially your own.

Even now, the journey continues. While I've made meaningful progress, I still face moments of struggle—with my body, with my habits, with the inner voice that questions whether I'm doing enough. But here's the truth: I'm still showing up. I'm still learning to be kind to myself. And I'm still working with Andrew (ten years later!) to build sustainable habits that support my health—not just for the short term, but for life. Together, we're focused on creating a rhythm of nutrition and movement that feels less like a crash course and more like a lifestyle. One grounded in consistency, self-respect, and grace.

> "Forgive yourself; you are not perfect.
> Show yourself grace; you are still learning.
> Show yourself patience; you are on a journey."
> — Shannon Yvette Tanner

## Are You Holding Yourself Back?

You deserve the same kindness and patience you so freely give to others. Before we can offer grace outward, we must learn to provide it to ourselves— and for many of us, that's the hardest place to start.

- Do you treat yourself with the same compassion you offer to others?
- When you make mistakes, do you use them as fuel to grow or as proof to shame yourself?
- Are you extending grace to the people you lead or love, allowing them to learn through experience?
- Do you equate your value with your performance or productivity?
- Are your expectations of yourself human—or superhuman?

Sometimes, we hold ourselves to a higher standard than others expect. We demand perfection, punish missteps, and push ourselves so hard that we forget that growth is a winding road, not a straight line. And when we internalize the idea that every slip-up is a failure, we rob ourselves of the ability to grow with gentleness. The truth is, grace is not weakness. Grace is strength wrapped in compassion.

## Building the Skill: Practicing Grace with Others and Yourself

Grace is not just a feeling—it's a choice we make over and over again. It's a mindset and practice that takes shape through our habits, leadership, and how we speak to ourselves. Whether you're navigating a tough conversation, recovering from a setback, or simply trying to be kinder to your own reflection, grace can become a steady guide. These strategies will help you lead and live with more grace, starting within and radiating outward.

1. **Reframe mistakes as lessons.**
   Every mistake is a data point, not a dead end. When someone on your team makes an error, or when you do, pause. Ask: "What can we learn from this?" Growth starts here.
2. **Offer encouragement, not just criticism.**
   Whether in leadership, friendship, or self-talk, grace means recognizing effort, not just outcomes. Acknowledge progress. Praise perseverance. And be the voice that says, "You're doing great. Keep going."
3. **Set realistic expectations.**
   It's easy to expect yourself to do it all—and do it perfectly. But grace reminds us that we are human. Set goals that challenge you, yes, but leave room for imperfection. You don't have to get it right every time. Setting grounded and realistic expectations can empower you to feel more in control and confident.
4. **Practice compassionate self-talk.**
   Would you talk to a friend the way you sometimes speak to yourself? Begin noticing your inner dialogue and take action to shift it from harsh to helpful. You deserve kindness—especially from yourself.
5. **Recognize progress, not only perfection.**
   Celebrate small wins. Whether it's sticking to a workout plan for a week, giving a difficult presentation, or setting a boundary in a relationship— acknowledge what you've done well. For instance, if you've been trying to eat healthier, instead of focusing on the days you "cheated," celebrate

the days you stuck to your plan. This shift in focus will help you recognize your progress and build your self-confidence. (Another nod to my trainer, Andrew.)

6. **Lead with empathy.**

   Give your team, family, peers, and friends the benefit of the doubt. Leading with grace means assuming good intent, listening openly, and correcting with kindness. This approach fosters a sense of connection and understanding.

Practicing grace doesn't mean you let things slide or lower your standards—it means you choose to meet life with presence, patience, and self-respect. As you incorporate these habits, remember that you are building more than resilience. You're building a new relationship with yourself and the people around you—one rooted in trust, kindness, and emotional strength. Give yourself permission to grow at your own pace. That is grace in action.

## Final Roar

*Grace is not something we master and move on from.*
*It's something we return to—*
*daily, gently, and intentionally.*

For me, it began with recognizing the voice in my head and deciding to speak back with love. It continued with asking for help, committing to growth, and learning to see progress where I used to see only flaws. And it continues now, as I create a new relationship with health, worth, and self-compassion.
*I will give myself grace.*
*I will keep showing up.*
*I will honor this body, this breath, this journey—*
*with kindness and care.*

# Authentic

## What It Means to Be Authentic

The word authentic comes from the Latin *autenticus*, meaning "original, genuine, true to oneself". And for me, it's not just a word—it's a core part of my identity. If there's one descriptor I want people to use when they talk about me, it's this: authentic.

What does being authentic mean to me? It means I am always honest. Always open. I speak my mind. I don't hold back. Most of all, I am always true to myself. I never try to pretend to be something I'm not. I'm not into masks or watered-down versions of me. You will always get the really real version—unfiltered, and sometimes a little intense.

Honestly, I've often felt like Jim Carrey in *Liar, Liar*—completely incapable of lying, even if it would make things easier. That character's over-the-top inability to filter his thoughts is meant for comedy, but I relate to it in a real way. I struggle even to tell a "soft lie" or a "partial truth." It's just not in me. And that's both a strength and a challenge. Because here's the twist: I don't like conflict. I try to avoid it. But I've realized that I avoid conflict not because I'm afraid of it, but because I know that if I do have to confront someone, I won't sugarcoat it. I'll speak my truth, and I'll speak it straight because I don't know how to do it any other way. And the truth is, conflict can be harsh—and I care about people, so I try to protect them from it.

That's the tension I live with: wanting to be honest, but not wanting to hurt people in the process.

Being authentic means I don't twist myself to fit expectations. But it also means I sometimes carry the weight of honesty, because the truth isn't always convenient. Still, I wouldn't trade it.

In my first corporate job out of college, I learned what it meant to be penalized for being authentic and true to myself. I took a position with a small software development company with fewer than thirty employees. What drew me in during the interview process was the owner's emphasis on values, branding, and culture.

But over time, a different culture emerged—one that quietly rewarded pedigree over performance. The owner openly favored employees from prestigious engineering or technical schools. I had earned two bachelor's degrees—one in math and one in computer science—from a respected liberal arts college.

I was assigned as the team leader for a project that included several of the "chosen ones" from the elite schools the owner admired—many of whom, I would later learn, were earning *more than triple my salary*. And while compensation mattered, what mattered more was equity. I wasn't asking to be the highest-paid—I wanted to be recognized and respected, especially when I was the one holding the responsibility for the team's success.

When I finally asked the owner for a raise and a promotion, his response was blunt. He dismissed my education, downplayed my technical skills, and—without hesitation—implied that, as a woman, I simply couldn't measure up to the men on the team.

He told me I could keep leading the project—but he'd never match my pay to theirs. It was one man's opinion, yes—but it reflected a much larger pattern I would encounter throughout my career.

That moment didn't just anger me—it clarified something. *I could either shrink to stay safe or walk away with my integrity.*

> ***That day, I decided I would never shrink***
> ***to fit someone else's comfort level.***

Being authentic isn't always easy, but it is always a powerful catalyst for personal growth. It's about standing in your power and becoming the best version of yourself.

You might be surprised how often you shrink without even realizing it. You hold back your ideas in meetings. You downplay your passions around people who don't "get" you. You smile when something hurts because you don't want to seem "too much."

But here's the truth:

> *Every time you abandon a part of yourself*
> *to make someone else comfortable,*
> *you dilute your power.*

Being authentic doesn't mean being unfiltered in every situation. It means being intentional about staying connected to who you are, even if you're the only one in the room doing it.

If you've been hiding pieces of yourself, ask why. Whose approval are you chasing? And is the cost of that approval your self-respect?

You don't need to be a chameleon to be accepted.

You need to be *you* to feel free.

## Are You Holding Yourself Back?

Let's be honest—being authentic isn't always easy. It can feel risky. Vulnerable. Even dangerous in environments that reward conformity over courage. Sometimes we're afraid to be our full selves because we've been conditioned to believe that being too open, too honest, too much is something to tone down.

We learn to wear masks because it feels safer than showing up as our full selves.

We begin to filter.

We soften our edges.

We polish our truth until it no longer resembles who we really are.

And the worst part? We start to forget what authenticity even looks like—because *we've been shrinking ourselves to fit someone else's ideals for so long.*

But you deserve to be real. Not watered down. Not carefully packaged to meet expectations.

***You deserve to take up space***
***just as you are.***

Let's explore where you might be concealing your authenticity. Ask yourself:

- Where in my life am I editing or filtering myself to be accepted?
- What parts of me feel too "messy," "loud," or "different" to show?
- Have I ever stayed silent or pretended to agree just to avoid rocking the boat?
- Do I adjust my tone or delivery to make others feel more at ease?

These aren't easy questions, but they're powerful ones.

Because the moment you get honest with yourself is the moment you begin to reclaim your voice.

## Building the Skill: How to Show Up Authentically

So, how do we get there? How do we peel off the layers of performance and step fully into who we are?

Start small. Start honestly. Start now.

Here are some ways to build your capacity for authenticity:

1. **Notice when you self-edit.**
   Catch yourself mid-sentence when you're about to say what you think someone wants to hear. Then pause, breathe, and say what you actually mean.

2. **Practice expressing your truth with kindness.**
   Authenticity isn't about being blunt; it's about being real and respectful. You can speak your truth without burning bridges.
3. **Journal your unfiltered thoughts.**
   Not for anyone else—just for you. Ask: What do I really think about this? What would I do if I weren't afraid of judgment?
4. **Reclaim the word "too".**
   Too sensitive. Too bold. Too emotional. Too ambitious. These aren't flaws—they're facets of your humanity. Wear them with pride.
5. **Surround yourself with people who get it.**
   The more you're around others who value realness over performance, the easier it becomes to stay true to yourself.

Authenticity is not a destination—it's a daily decision. The more you choose to show up as your full self, the more ease, connection, and confidence you'll feel in every space you enter. These strategies aren't about becoming someone new—they're about coming home to who you've always been. Start small. Stay honest. And keep practicing the courage to be you.

## Final Roar

Pick one situation this week where you tend to shrink. Maybe it's a team meeting, a dinner with extended family, or a space where you usually go quiet. Before you walk in, say to yourself: *I have nothing to prove. I only have to be me.*

Then step into that space with your full presence.

Breathe.

And show up as the whole, honest, unedited version of yourself.

Because the real you is not just enough.

*She's powerful. She's worthy. She's unforgettable.*

The world doesn't need another perfectly curated version of womanhood.

The world needs *you*—raw, real and relentlessly authentic.

*"We teach girls to shrink themselves, to make themselves smaller.*
*We say to girls: 'You can have ambition, but not too much.'"*
— Chimamanda Ngozi Adichie

**I will no longer shrink to fit**
**someone else's expectations**
**of what I should be.**
**I am not a version of someone.**
**I am authentically me.**

# Refined

## What It Means to Be Refined

The word refined often conjures images of sophistication—polished manners, elegant fashion, perhaps even a glass of wine held just so. In fact, "to refine" comes from the Latin *refinare*, meaning "to purify"—to distill something down to its most essential, elevated form.

But in the context of empowerment, what does it really mean to be refined? It's not about being aloof or "too good" for others. True refinement is about being thoughtful, composed, and inclusive. It's about showing up in the world with grace, humility, and care—for yourself and for others, regardless of their background or circumstances.

Refined individuals have a discerning eye—not just for etiquette or aesthetics, but for humanity. They are respectful in their interactions, culturally aware, and always learning. To be refined, you don't have to be an art critic or a wine connoisseur. You simply need to present yourself with intention and treat others with dignity.

Being refined is not about perfection—it's a lifelong journey of self-awareness, learning, and connection. It's about choosing to grow, adapt, and meet people where they are—a journey that is both challenging and rewarding.

For me, the most refined people I've ever known were my parents. They opened their home—and their hearts—to people others had cast aside. I remember guests from all walks of life finding refuge under our roof. Each one was facing some sort of turmoil, though I didn't always understand the details at the time. But my parents never asked for explanations. There were no strings attached. They simply offered what was needed: *a roof, a warm meal, a moment to breathe, a sense of family*—and, always, *unconditional respect.*

They did this with grace, without fanfare, and without judgment. They were protectors of dignity. *That is the true essence of refinement.* I miss them every day, but I carry their example in my heart and try to embody it in how I show up for others.

Refinement is not about appearance or exclusivity. It's about acceptance, empathy, cultural intelligence, and love. And I hope that one day, the world will be refined in this way—where everyone is welcomed, seen, and valued.

## Are You Holding Yourself Back?

Many of us have been conditioned to associate refinement with status or perfection—things that feel unattainable or unrelatable. Maybe you've thought: *I'm not fancy enough*, or *That's just not who I am.* We assume that being refined means you must speak a certain way, dress a certain way, or exist in some exclusive realm that feels distant from our everyday lives.

But here's the truth: holding yourself back from refinement because you think it's only for the elite is a misunderstanding of what this word truly means.

You may be holding yourself back if you:

- Avoid opportunities to elevate your communication or presence for fear of seeming "fake" or "too much."
- Judge yourself harshly for not being familiar with cultural references, etiquette rules, or societal norms.
- Struggle with embracing others who are different from you, perhaps out of fear, bias, or unfamiliarity.
- Feel like you must hide parts of your story or background to "fit in" with a more "refined" crowd.

Refinement is not about changing who you are. *It's about evolving into the best version of yourself*—and having the courage to treat others with dignity and openness, no matter their background, experiences, perspectives, or differences.

Let go of the idea that refinement is about perfection or pretense. Instead, embrace it as a practice of thoughtful living, respect, and elevated presence. You don't have to have it all figured out. You just have to be willing to grow with grace.

## Building the Skill: How to Be Refined

So, how do you cultivate the empowering version of refined—the kind that uplifts others, honors your values, and reflects your inner strength?

Start with these empowering activities:

1. **Practice presence.**
   Refined individuals are intentional with their presence. That means listening deeply, maintaining eye contact, showing up on time, and being mindful of your words and actions. Words matter.
2. **Elevate your language.**
   You don't have to speak like royalty, but speaking with clarity, kindness, and confidence is a form of refinement. Avoid gossip, crude language, or negativity. Choose words that build bridges, not walls.
3. **Curate your surroundings.**
   This doesn't mean you need luxury. It means creating a space— physically and emotionally—that reflects what you value. Clean, intentional, welcoming spaces signal care and refinement.
4. **Celebrate culture and difference.**
   Make it a habit to learn about other cultures, traditions, and worldviews. Ask questions, listen without judgment, and find ways to connect across differences. Inclusion is refinement in action.

5. **Lead with grace.**

    Especially in challenging moments. Whether you're in a heated discussion or witnessing someone being mistreated, choose to rise above. Speak with conviction and truth, not condemnation or unchecked emotion.

6. **Honor your roots.**

    Like my parents did—be proud of where you come from and use your experiences to offer compassion to others. A refined person uplifts, supports, and shelters those who need it.

## Final Roar

I used to think being refined meant being above it all—detached, untouchable, perfect. Now I know better.

>*Refinement is found in the quiet strength*
>*of those who open their doors,*
>*listen with intention,*
>*and meet people with dignity,*
>*regardless of their differences.*

It's choosing respect over ridicule, curiosity over judgment, and grace over ego. It's meeting people where they are, not forcing them to conform to our way of thinking.

My parents lived that truth every single day. They showed me that refinement isn't about being impressive—it's about being impactful.

And that's what I carry forward.

*To be refined is to be a safe place in a chaotic world.*

*To be refined is to walk through life with empathy, elegance, and compassion.*

*To be refined is to choose love—on purpose, every single time.*

My parents' legacy lives in me—and it can live in you, too.

# Unique

## What It Means to Be Unique

The word *unique* comes from the Latin *unicus*, meaning "one of a kind." And for most of my life, I've wrestled with that—not because I didn't want to be different, but because I didn't always want to be *seen* as different.

Growing up, there was an unspoken path—one that many in my extended family followed. My parents, brother, sister-in-law, cousins, aunts, and uncles had all gone to the same small college, Greenville College, a Free Methodist school with a strong legacy. The expectation was clear: this was where "the Gines kids" went. But deep down, I knew I needed something different. Not because I didn't love or respect my family or our heritage—I did—but because I didn't want to be seen as just another "Gines."

And my big brother may not even know this—I especially didn't want to be seen at that college as just his little sister.

I wanted to carve my own path.

I ended up attending Taylor University, a non-denominational Christian college, and from the beginning, I never really felt like I fit neatly into any one category.

I wasn't the party girl. I wasn't the legacy student. I wasn't the one with a clear "path."

I was the one buried in textbooks—taking tough courses in math and computer science, juggling odd jobs just to stay afloat. I didn't qualify for the campus work-study program, so I pieced things together however I could.

On paper, I was a total nerd—organized, analytical, tech-savvy to the core. But then there was the other side of me—the side that came alive on stage, singing in an all-female music group, harmonizing and playing the piano with joy and presence.

I was logic *and* lyric. Passion *and* precision.

I even broke the mold in my relationships.

During college, I dated someone who didn't quite "fit" the expectations of those around me. We were in different social circles, different classes, and yes—different stages of life. But I knew there was something real between us, even if others couldn't see it.

For the first time, I stopped looking outward for approval. I trusted my own heart. I knew what I brought to the table, and I knew what I needed. That was enough.

Looking back, I realize I spent a lot of those years floating between spaces—not quite fitting in with the artists, or the science students, or the campus socialites. But somewhere between the spreadsheets and the sheet music, I found something more powerful than belonging: I found myself.

I didn't need to fit a category. I was the category.

Years later, that same energy would define my leadership style in the workplace. I once led a major business integration project that blended two clashing teams. The tension was thick—nobody wanted to be there. So I brought in a silly mascot, turned each project milestone into a fun game, and created a collaborative scoreboard with mini-challenges and bragging rights. It was unconventional. It was unexpected.

And it worked.

That project was a turning point—not just because it succeeded, but because it reminded me that my way of doing things *was* the strategy.

I didn't have to lead like anyone else. I could lead like me.

That's the part no one teaches you: your uniqueness isn't a quirk to be managed. It's your *edge*. Your essence. And the truth is, you're not just one of a kind—you're **one of one**.

There will never be another person with your exact mix of gifts, grit, wisdom, humor, scars, dreams, and vision. Not now. Not ever.

That means whatever you create, speak, build, love, or lead will carry your fingerprint.

So why do we keep trying to shrink ourselves to fit what already exists—when we were born to invent something that doesn't exist yet?

Being unique means bringing your full, unfiltered self into every room you enter.

*When you learn to embrace your uniqueness,*
*it becomes a superpower.*

And if I'm being honest, I didn't always see my uniqueness as a strength. For years, I tried hard to blend in—muting my personality, shrinking my ideas, and chasing the illusion of "normal." But I've learned that chasing normal isn't my path. It's not the goal. Because "normal" doesn't light me up—and it doesn't spark the kind of change I want to influence.

Today, I don't just accept what makes me different—I honor it and embrace it. I realize that my path may be unconventional, my ideas may be bold, and my energy might take up more space than expected—but that's exactly what sets me apart. I don't enter rooms hoping to fit in. I walk in ready to light them up and fill the space with all of me and my uniqueness. I want that for you, too.

## Are You Holding Yourself Back?

It's easy to want to blend in. Standing out can feel risky, and for many of us, it's something we've been taught to avoid. We silence our quirks, hide our interests, and shrink ourselves just enough to fit in more comfortably.

Have you ever caught yourself:

- Avoiding leadership roles because your style felt different from what others expected?
- Feeling ashamed of past choices because they didn't follow the "typical" path?

- Pretending to like or agree with something to keep the peace?
- Dismissing your own ideas because they felt "too out there"?

You're not alone. But here's the truth: *The world doesn't need more sameness. It needs you*—your story, your perspective, your flair. You don't need to follow a blueprint. You are the blueprint.

## Building the Skill: Embracing Your Uniqueness

Your uniqueness isn't just something to accept—it's something to *practice*. Like any empowering trait, learning to live fully as yourself takes intention, courage, and consistency. It means allowing yourself to lead, express, and show up in ways that might defy expectations—but feel profoundly true.

The following strategies will help you amplify that superpower and embrace what sets you apart with clarity, confidence, and joy.

1. **Reframe "different" as "distinct."**
   Write down five ways you've felt "different" in your life. Now, go back and reword each one to make it reflect something powerful or positive. For example, *I always questioned authority* becomes *I am a natural critical thinker.* Or, *I was the quiet one in school* becomes *I'm a thoughtful observer who listens deeply.*

2. **Own your story—all of it.**
   Instead of hiding your experiences, share them. Talk about your unconventional choices, your strange hobbies, your zig-zag career path. Every twist in your story adds depth and dimension to who you are, and sharing it can help others feel connected and understood.

3. **Infuse your personality into your work.**
   Like the project mascot I introduced, consider how you can make your leadership, creativity, or communication style your own. What brings you joy? What energizes a room? What's your signature move? My signature move is to amplify my former cheerleader persona— sometimes literally—by bringing out physical pom-poms.

4. **Surround yourself with open minds.**

Spend time with people who celebrate your quirks, not just tolerate them. Community is powerful, but the right community will remind you how special your individuality truly is.

5. **Lead by example.**

When you unapologetically show up as your full self, you give others permission to do the same. That's how cultures shift. That's how people grow.

Your uniqueness is a leadership advantage—don't underestimate it. Whenever you choose to lead from your authentic core, you model something bold and freeing for others. These strategies aren't about fitting in. They're about standing fully in who you are and trusting that who you are is more than enough.

## Final Roar

You weren't made to blend in. You were made to stand out.

Your uniqueness is your superpower—and the world needs what only you can bring. There is no one else on this earth with your voice, your story, your spark.

You are not a copy.

You are an original masterpiece.

*So walk boldly, speak freely,*
*and live as the fullest expression of yourself.*
*Because being different isn't a weakness—*
*it's your greatest strength.*

*I am one of one.*
*I am enough, exactly as I am.*
*I am unique, and that is my superpower.*

# Worthy

## What It Means to Be Worthy

The word worthy comes from the Old English *weorþ*, meaning "honorable" or "deserving of respect." It's a powerful reminder that worth isn't something we have to earn or prove. It's something we already have. But let's be honest—how often do we actually believe that?

When I think of the word worthy, I immediately think of self-worth and the profound struggle many of us face in owning it. We live in a fast-paced, digitally saturated world where social media often becomes a source of validation. Platforms designed to connect us have turned into comparison traps and highlight reels, where "likes" have become substitutes for self-worth. It's easy to forget that our value doesn't come from a screen or a metric—our value comes from within.

Every single person deserves to be recognized, not just for their accomplishments, but for who they are. That includes you. That includes the work you've done, the effort you've given, the boundaries you've set, and the obstacles you've overcome. It includes the unseen moments—the ones no one claps for.

As leaders, especially, we become so obsessed with chasing goals, hitting metrics, and supporting others that we often forget to pause and honor our own journey. We forget to celebrate our own small victories, the ones that add up to real growth.

Part of my self-care regimen is to remind myself daily: *I am worthy of recognition.* But I didn't always do this. I have an inner critic who used to whisper—sometimes scream—that I wasn't enough. For years, I struggled with self-confidence. I dismissed my efforts and minimized my accomplishments. It took decades of reflection, therapy, and growth to quiet those voices. But now, in my 50s, I finally see my worth clearly. I honor it. I protect it.

Years ago, I worked for a company ahead of its time in the field of artificial intelligence. We had developed a sophisticated underwriting engine that automated insurance policy evaluations—groundbreaking work destined to reshape the industry.

My first assignment was a high-stakes client implementation. The sales team had drastically underestimated the scope, promising delivery in just a few months. In truth, it required more than four full person-years of effort. Our small team of three gave nearly a year of our lives to that project. We worked 12 to 16 hours a day, seven days a week. I temporarily relocated hundreds of miles from home, leaving my now ex-husband behind. I gained 35 pounds. I lost my joy. And all I could think was, *Just keep pushing—get it done.*

And we did. Against all odds, we delivered. It was a massive success—a game-changer for the project and our team.

But when it was all over, the recognition didn't match the personal sacrifices we made as a team. A modest bonus. A quiet thank-you. No public credit. No true celebration.

For years, I clung to the belief that good work would speak for itself. That if I kept my head down, stayed humble, and didn't ask for praise, someone would eventually notice. But the truth is—waiting for someone else to validate your worth is a losing game. Because worth doesn't live in titles or thank-yous or performance reviews.

**Worth is not something you earn.**
**It's something you own.**

That moment cracked something open in me. I stopped waiting to be seen. I stopped tying my value to someone else's ability—or inability—to acknowledge it. I gave my notice, moved on to a better job, and made a quiet vow I still live by today:

**I will no longer outsource my worth.**

That was the beginning of my self-worth revolution. I no longer measure myself by external applause. I honor the effort, not just the outcome. I notice the growth. I celebrate the quiet wins. And I remind myself daily:

**I am worthy—not because of what I do, but because of who I am.**

This chapter isn't about becoming worthy. It's about remembering that you already are. Your worth doesn't increase with achievements, and it doesn't decrease with mistakes. It just *is*—constant, unwavering, and fully yours.

You are worthy—in all your lioness beauty. Always have been. Always will be.

Now, I make daily recognition a non-negotiable part of my self-care. I pause and ask, *What did I accomplish today—big or small?* Then I speak it out loud:

- "I answered a tough email today."
- "I had a hard conversation."
- "I said no without guilt."
- "I asked for help when I needed it."
- "I showed up even when I didn't want to."

And then I say the magic words: *I am worthy of celebrating this.*
Because I am. And so are you.

## Are You Holding Yourself Back?

So many of us are. We shrug off our successes. We minimize our magic. We act like getting through the day isn't an achievement—when in fact, *have you tried adulting lately?!* In a world of 30-second sound bites and constant noise, being present, getting out of bed, caring for yourself or others—that's not small. That's survival. That's worthy.

But we've been conditioned to believe our worth is tied to productivity, appearance, and approval. We wait to feel "enough" until someone else hands us that stamp of validation. That mindset? It keeps us small. It teaches us to play quietly when we want to roar. And it's time to unlearn that narrative.

Let's begin shifting your mindset around worth with these questions:

- Do I give more recognition to others than I do to myself?
- Do I only feel worthy when I'm achieving, performing, or meeting expectations?
- Do I downplay my accomplishments out of fear of seeming arrogant?

Know this: if you answered yes to any of these questions, you're not alone. And you're not broken. But you may be withholding the power of your own self-recognition—and that's a form of self-betrayal. One that I want to help you dismantle. Maybe you've said these things to yourself:

- *That wasn't a big deal.*
- *Anyone could've done it.*
- *It wasn't perfect.*

Sound familiar? This is your inner critic chipping away at your sense of self-worth. That inner critic needs to be silenced. Those comments reinforce the false belief that only the extraordinary counts.

But here's the truth: you don't need to be extraordinary to be worthy. You just need to be honest. Human. Present. And willing to show up.

*The woman who makes space for herself*
*in a noisy world*
*is already doing something*
*extraordinary.*

# Building the Skill: How to Root Yourself in Worthiness

Let's flip the script for a minute. I want to propose a challenge that will help you recognize how often you allow your inner critic to downplay your successes. For the next 7 days, name <u>one win</u> at the end of each day. Any size. Any kind. Say it out loud:

**"I accomplished _____ today. I am worthy of celebrating this."**

Then, take it one step further: give yourself a literal pat on the back or a Mel Robbins' high-five in the mirror. Smile. Stand tall. Let the worthiness settle into your bones.

Here are a few more ways to reinforce your worth:

1. **Start a "Worthy Wins" journal.**
   Write just one line a day. Don't overthink it—just capture the moment. Let it be proof that you're showing up.
2. **Celebrate the "imperfect" wins.**
   Maybe you said "no" when you usually say "yes." Or you rested when you felt guilty. That counts. Those are wins rooted in growth.
3. **Create a "Worthy Wall."**
   Use sticky notes, a whiteboard, or a mirror to track your wins and affirmations where you can see them. Watch that wall grow into a visual reminder of your value.
4. **Write a love letter to your past self.**
   Tell her what you're proud of. Acknowledge her strengths, her choices, and her survival.

5. **Post notes on your mirror.**

   Give yourself visible cues to remind yourself how amazing you are. Notes like **"I am worthy."** and **"I celebrate me."** These affirmations can help you shift your mindset. Read them every morning and every night until you truly believe them.

6. **Give yourself daily reminders.**

   You are not your to-do list. You are not your income. You are not your likes. You are worthy because you exist. Period.

## Final Roar

I will no longer outsource my worth.
I don't need applause to know I matter.
I don't need validation to take up space.
I don't need permission to rise.
My worth is not defined by titles, praise, or approval.
It's etched in my presence, my resilience, and my roar.
I was born worthy.

*And I will rise like a lioness*
*who finally remembers her roar—*
*and the world cannot silence me*
*anymore.*

# II

# Ignite the Spark

# Energy, Joy, and Passion

There's a fire within every woman—an inner light that, when kindled, radiates warmth, creativity, and vitality. This part of the book is about tapping into that energy source, not just to feel more alive, but to live more fully. The words you'll explore in Part II—like *Vivacious, Passionate, Feisty,* and *Audacious*—are not about being loud or over-the-top. They're about reconnecting with joy, owning your energy, and expressing your fire—your way.

Too often, women are taught to dim their light. We're told not to be too enthusiastic, too joyful, too much. We're encouraged to shrink, to soften our presence, to be cautious instead of bold. That conditioning often causes us to second-guess our instincts, withhold our enthusiasm, or refrain from expressing our full selves. We become afraid of being labeled "too much" or "not enough" all at once. But the truth is, our spark is not a liability—it's our superpower.

This section is your permission slip to reclaim your spark. These are words that energize—words that give you permission to play, to express, to risk, to radiate. These words will remind you that joy is not a luxury—it's a birthright. And energy isn't something you have to chase; it's something you can cultivate by aligning with your purpose, your curiosity, and your desires.

Let these words be fuel. Let them reignite the parts of you that have gone quiet or grown dim. Let them remind you that passion is not only powerful—it's necessary. It's the driving force behind your boldest dreams and deepest fulfillment.

Because when a woman chooses to live audaciously, to express joy freely, and to own her energy fully, she becomes an unstoppable force. People feel her presence the moment she enters the room. Like Rihanna sings—*shine bright like a diamond.*

Let's go be beautiful—like diamonds in the sky.

# Audacious

## What It Means to Be Audacious

*Audacious.* Just saying the word makes your heart beat a little faster.

Audacious means extremely bold, daring, recklessly brave, and unbound by conventional ideas or norms. It comes from the Latin word *audere*, meaning "to dare." Over time, the word has sometimes picked up a negative connotation, suggesting someone is rude, brazen, or disrespectful. But I see it differently.

For me, being audacious means *choosing courage over comfort, boldness over hesitation*, and most importantly, *self-trust over societal expectation*. It means deciding to live out loud—to go after the things you want even when you're not 100% sure how it will all turn out.

I was reminded of this in a very real way years ago when my department underwent a significant reorganization, and suddenly, boldness wasn't just a mindset. It was a necessity. I had been in my current role for several years. There were four people at the same senior position level: three men and me. As part of the reorganization, three new teams were being formed—three new leadership positions—and I was the odd "woman" out.

Despite being highly qualified to lead one of those teams—by all accounts, *the* most skilled—I was told I wouldn't be given the opportunity. Why? Because my male peers were encouraged to "stretch" and grow into the role—while I was told I didn't need the opportunity, since everyone already knew I could do it. Instead, I was asked to help coach and mentor the very men who were chosen over me.

Let that sink in.

I was being sidelined—not for lack of ability, but because my excellence was being used against me. It wasn't right. It wasn't fair. And it certainly wasn't okay with me.

So I decided to be audacious. I went to my HR representative and said, "I need help finding a new role." She mentioned a new project that was in its very early stages, one that would require relocating if I wanted to participate.

Without hesitation, I said, "Sign me up." No flinching. No second-guessing. Just a bold, fearless *yes*.

That decision changed my career trajectory—and reminded me what I'm capable of when I trust my own value. I didn't ask for permission. I didn't wait for someone to rescue me. I took the reins of my destiny in my own hands. I moved. Audaciously.

That moment still grounds me today. And when I feel my confidence waver, I return to the practice of writing *intention statements*—short, powerful affirmations that help me anchor my worth and my direction.

Here's one I come back to often:

*I am a brave, bold, daring person*
*who is not afraid to push against my comfort zone*
*to strive for my goals with audacity.*

Writing intention statements gives me clarity and focus. They're not fluff. They're declarations. And they help me stay connected to the fire inside me.

Now it's your turn. What would your audacious intention statement sound like?

## Are You Holding Yourself Back?

Let's get real.

Being audacious can feel unnatural, especially if you've spent years trying to "get it right," not ruffle feathers, or fit in. While we often admire bold people from afar, we hesitate when it comes to ourselves.

Why?

Because somewhere along the way, we were taught to *play small*. To wait for our turn. To ask for permission. We were told to be polite, not powerful. To be cautious, not courageous. And now, even when we dream bigger, we feel guilty for wanting more.

Our inner voice starts whispering:

- *What if I fail?*
- *What will people think?*
- *I'm not ready yet.*

That voice of doubt? It's not truth. It's conditioning. It's the echo of every moment we were taught that being *too much* was something to avoid.

Here's the shift: You can be humble *and* audacious, kind *and* bold, and take up space without apology. It's an "and" proposition, not an "either/or."

Remember: audacity is not arrogance. It's *ownership*.

So, are you holding yourself back? Or are you ready to step forward with the fire that's already inside you?

## Building the Skill: Audacity in Action

Ready to own your boldness? These steps will help you unlock your inner audacity—one intentional action at a time.

1. **Challenge your comfort zone—intentionally.**
   You don't have to do something outrageous to be audacious. You just need to take one small step beyond your usual. Speak up in a meeting. Say yes to something that scares you. Dare to try before you feel ready.
2. **Write your intention statement—and live by it.**
   What do you want to believe about yourself? Write it in the present tense. Be specific. Speak it out loud. Post it where you'll see it. Your intention becomes your internal compass.

3. **Flip the fear script.**

   Instead of *What if I fail?*, ask *What if this changes everything?* Reframe the scary "what ifs" into possibilities. Let hope carry as much weight as fear.

4. **Take imperfect, unapologetic action.**

   Stop waiting until everything is perfectly aligned. Audacity doesn't require a detailed map—it just needs a spark. Start messy. Move forward. Adjust as you go.

5. **Surround yourself with audacity.**

   Who do you admire for their boldness? Learn from them. Spend time with people who expand your thinking, support your courage, and show you what's possible.

*Being audacious doesn't require you to be fearless—*
*it requires you to be faithful to your own power.*

Every small act of bravery you take strengthens your audacity mindset. You don't have to shout to be bold. Sometimes the most audacious thing you can do is quietly refuse to shrink.

## Final Roar

You don't need anyone's permission to go after what sets your soul on fire.

Let this be the moment you stop asking "Can I?" and start declaring "Watch me." You are not too much. You are not too bold. You are not too ambitious. You are exactly as daring, capable, and powerful as you were meant to be.

*I am brave. I am bold.*
*I am daring. I am audacious.*
*And I will no longer shrink*
*to fit into spaces I've outgrown.*

# Feisty

## What It Means to Be Feisty

The word feisty often conjures images of small-but-mighty women—those who speak up, fight back, and bring bold energy into every room they enter. When I looked up the formal definition—"typically of a person who is relatively small or weak"—I couldn't help but laugh. I may be vertically challenged, sure. But weak? Not a chance. Feisty isn't about size or stature—it's about strength of character, determination, and the courage to speak your truth, even when it's not the popular opinion.

When I call myself feisty, I'm saying I know exactly who I am. I speak up. I stand my ground. And I don't back down. I will fight fiercely and passionately for what I believe is right. But society doesn't always view feisty women this way. In fact, the word is often misinterpreted—seen as overly aggressive, emotional, or even unruly, especially in the workplace. And that is when unconscious biases creep in.

*Unconscious bias* refers to the deeply embedded stereotypes and assumptions we all carry—often without realizing it. These biases shape how we perceive assertiveness, leadership, and emotion. A confident man is perceived as strong. A confident woman? She's often called bossy, aggressive, or emotional. Feisty women challenge these biases daily—simply by refusing to be silenced.

And I will not be silenced. So I embrace it. I own it. I've learned that being feisty is necessary, especially in male-dominated industries. Several times in my career, I saw male colleagues being promoted around me, despite what I believed was comparable—or even stronger—performance on my part. Instead of stewing in silence, I presented my case to my manager and asked plainly: "What do I need to do to get a promotion?" His answer? He didn't know. So I kept asking. I documented our conversations. I followed up. Finally, he asked me to stop asking because he did not have an answer for me—and wouldn't have one anytime soon. That's when I realized the truth: my career was my responsibility. That moment—fueled by fire and feistiness—taught me I was done waiting for a system not designed to elevate me. So I started showing up differently—more direct, more vocal, and unwilling to be dismissed.

One moment I'll never forget occurred during a leadership meeting, where I voiced strong concerns about the direction of a project. I wasn't combative—I was prepared, clear, and confident. But the minute I finished speaking, a senior male colleague leaned back in his chair and chuckled. "Well, someone's feeling feisty today," he said, with a smirk that dismissed everything I'd just said.

In that moment, I felt a familiar tension rise in my chest—the urge to shrink, to laugh it off, to smooth things over. But instead, I held eye contact and replied, "Feisty is one word for it. Passionate. Prepared. Unafraid to challenge bad decisions—those work too."

There was a beat of silence. Then, a few quiet nods around the room. The topic moved on, but I didn't. I walked out of that meeting knowing this:

1. I had just taught someone how to treat me.
2. I wouldn't apologize for being a woman with an opinion.

That day didn't make me feisty. It reminded me that I already was—and that feistiness wasn't a flaw to fix. It was the fire that fueled my leadership.

*Feisty women don't wait for permission.*
*We act. We advocate.*
*We own our power.*

## Are You Holding Yourself Back?

In the 17th century, conduct books written by men outlined the "ideal" behavior for women. A common directive? That women should be seen and not heard. Even today, this outdated belief lingers—especially in the workplace, where the unspoken expectation often still is: Don't speak too loudly. Don't take up too much space.

Well, I refuse to be quiet.

I push back—intentionally—when challenged for speaking up too much. I proudly describe myself as feisty or sassy, because I want it to be known: I will always stand up for what I believe in. And I will always fight to make sure women have a voice at the table.

Here are some common ways you may be holding yourself back from being the feisty woman you were born to be:

- Have you been taught to "tone it down" when you show passion or conviction?
- Do you fear speaking up because you're worried you'll be labeled as difficult or emotional?
- Do you feel the pressure to be "nurturing" or "easygoing" when your spirit screams to be bold, brave, and honest?

If you've ever silenced yourself to stay palatable or avoid conflict, you might be holding back your inner feisty fire. There is power in being strong-willed and self-assured. There is value in asking the hard questions and refusing to settle for vague answers.

*Don't let the fear of being misunderstood*
*keep you from standing up*
*and standing out.*

# Building the Skill: Strategies to Embrace Your Feisty Side

Being feisty is not just who you are; it's how you rise. These strategies will help you step fully into that fierce energy, unapologetically own your power, and show the world precisely what happens when a woman stops holding back.

1. **Redefine the word.**
   Write your own definition of "feisty." Let it reflect your strength, courage, and passion—not someone else's outdated perception. Post your "feisty" definition on your mirror, on the steering wheel of your car, on your coffee maker, or even your monitor at work. Don't be afraid to remind yourself that feisty is a positive trait.

2. **Advocate for yourself.**
   Practice speaking up in safe spaces, such as with trusted friends or mentors. Then apply that courage in real conversations at work or in life where your voice needs to be heard.

3. **Document your wins.**
   Keep a record of your accomplishments and the efforts you make. When the time comes to advocate for a raise, promotion, or opportunity, you'll have the receipts.

4. **Reframe feedback.**
   If someone calls you "too intense" or "too much," ask yourself: Is this a reflection of my power or their discomfort?

5. **Encourage other feisty women.**
   When you see another woman standing her ground, cheer her on. Normalize assertiveness as a strength, not a flaw.

*Your fire was never meant to be hidden—*
*it was meant to lead, inspire,*
*and shake things up.*

# Final Roar

Even in the face of criticism or opposition, don't let anyone extinguish your passion or deter you from speaking your truth.

Being feisty isn't a flaw. It's a force.

Let them call you too much. Too loud. Too emotional. Too assertive.

That just means they felt your heat.

And that heat? That's your power burning through the walls they tried to build around you.

Whenever I need to reignite my inner fire, I listen to *Fight Song* by Rachel Platten—especially the line:

*"I might only have one match, but I can make an explosion."*

That lyric hits me right in the soul. Being feisty means knowing that you still stand your ground even if the odds are stacked against you. You still speak your truth. You ignite change with nothing but your voice, your passion, and your persistence.

You don't need an army to make a difference—you just need the guts to light the match.

Don't shrink. Don't soften. Don't silence your spark.

*Fan it. Feed it. Let it roar.*

> **To every woman who's been told**
> **to be quiet, calm down,**
> **or stop making waves—**
> **light the fire anyway.**

# Vivacious

## What It Means to Be Vivacious

The word vivacious stems from the Latin *vivax*, meaning "lively" or "long-lived," with roots in *vivere*—the verb for "to live". And oh, do I believe in living—fully. Vivaciousness isn't just about being upbeat or bubbly. It's about bringing a spark into the room. It's the kind of energy that lifts people up, turns ordinary moments into celebrations, and reminds everyone around you that life is meant to be felt. Being vivacious is about choosing vitality and choosing light. Choosing to show up—even when the world wants you to quiet down.

When I think of what it means to be vivacious, I think of someone vibrant, larger-than-life, the center of attention, or the life of the party. As an extrovert, being vivacious fits naturally with my personality. I don't need to be the center of attention, but I do love being the one who can cheer up a group or shift the vibe of a room simply by walking in.

In leadership, being vivacious means being present—*really* present—as you guide your team through challenging projects, tight deadlines, and complex problems. It means showing up confidently, enthusiastically, and with a calming sense of certainty. When I lead a team, I want my team to feel proud, protected, and supported. I become the mama bear—the one people must go through to get to my team. Not around me. *Through* me.

But here's the thing: being vivacious isn't about being loud. It's about being attentive, supportive, and anchored. It means you're the one holding things together, picking up the slack, setting the tone. You're the strongest link in the chain—the one who lifts others up when they falter.

But I'll be honest—there have been seasons in my life when I didn't feel vivacious at all. I wasn't the strongest link. I wasn't showing up the way I wanted to for my team, or even for myself. Life has a way of piling on—work stress, personal setbacks, just the everyday pressure of being an adult. It happens. And when I'm not bringing my usual spark, it doesn't just affect me. Others feel it too. Energy is contagious, and when mine is off, the ripple effect can shift an entire team's mood.

Through many challenging experiences, I've learned to recognize the signs when my energy levels dip. I don't always succeed, but I've learned to pause, regroup, and utilize the tools I've built to shift back into a more grounded, vibrant state. Vivaciousness isn't about perfection—it's about presence. And presence starts with self-awareness, empowering us to take control of our energy and bring our best selves to every interaction.

One of the most challenging times of my life came during a complex project where everything seemed to go wrong—delays, cost overruns, and no end in sight. I worked 60–70 hours a week and still couldn't keep up. My usually vivacious flame had dimmed to a flicker, and eventually, just a glowing ember. I had always prided myself on being the spark—the one who lifted others up. But in that moment, I had lost my ability to influence the team—or even enjoy the work. I dreaded coming to work every morning. I felt powerless.

I remember confiding in the project manager—someone I trusted and respected—and telling him I was burned out and considering moving on to another project that had come my way. I was frustrated and needed something different. He understood and was gracious enough to agree to work on a transition plan with me. Initially, we developed a 3- to 4-month roll-off plan. But a few days later, he called me at home after work and said, "I need you to go now." He told me he cared too much about me to watch me keep going when I had clearly lost my spark.

That moment hit me hard. He saw what I couldn't admit to myself: I wasn't me anymore. I wasn't smiling. I was short-tempered, frustrated, and drained. I was unhappy. My home life was suffering. I was barely holding it together, and didn't want to "let go". That meant giving up—I am not a quitter.

The *courage* of that project manager—to let me go before I completely broke down and fell apart—gave me the space I needed to heal.

To that project manager—if you're reading this, you know who you are. Thank you for having the courage to speak the truth I couldn't yet admit. Letting me go wasn't easy, but it was exactly what I needed. You helped me protect my mental health at a time when I was quietly unraveling. You saw me, and you saved me from losing myself. Thank you.

Slowly, I began to rebuild. I gave myself time to rest, reflect, and reconnect with what brings me joy. That smoldering ember? I nurtured it back into a flame. And eventually, my vivacious energy came roaring back.

Sharing this story isn't just about reflection—it's about illumination. What I'm doing in these pages is more than writing—I'm revisiting a turning point that shaped me. And if you're reading this while going through your own season of burnout or feeling like your light has dimmed, I want you to know: you're not alone. I've been there. I see you. And I hope that by sharing my story, I can help light the path for someone else who may be quietly struggling, just like I once was.

And while I identify as an extrovert, I want to clarify that vivaciousness isn't reserved for the loudest person in the room. Introverts can absolutely be vivacious too—through quiet enthusiasm, magnetic presence, or a joyful energy that radiates from within. Being vivacious is less about volume and more about vitality. It's the spark in your eye, the passion in your work, and the authenticity you bring to every interaction, no matter how big or small. It's a quality that transcends personality types, making everyone feel accepted and valued for their unique energy.

I've always been the cheerleader. On more than one project, I've literally brought pom poms into the office. When we have a win—even a small one—I raise those pom poms and let out a loud "Yay!" Do I get eye rolls? You bet. Do I care? Not at all. Because behind those eye rolls are the smiles and laughter that tell me my team feels seen and supported. They know it's not a gimmick—it's real. It's me.

*I live my life out loud. Vivaciously. Because life is meant to be enjoyed.*

## Are You Holding Yourself Back?

Sometimes we suppress our vivacious spirit to fit in or avoid judgment. Were you ever told to "calm down," "stop being so extra," or "take it down a notch"? Those words can plant seeds of self-doubt. Over time, you might start second-guessing your natural joy, muting your light to make others more comfortable.

Society doesn't always reward women for being vivacious. We get labeled as "too much," "too emotional," or "unprofessional" for expressing joy or energy. There's often this unspoken rule that in order to be respected, you have to be reserved. But that rule wasn't written with us in mind—and it certainly doesn't serve us. When we dull our energy, we don't just betray ourselves—we rob others of the light we bring into the room.

Ask yourself:

- Do I ever dim my personality to avoid standing out too much?
- Have I ever felt guilty for being "too much" or "too loud"?
- Do I associate fun, playfulness, or high energy with being unprofessional?

If you answered yes to any of those, you may be holding yourself back from your vivacious nature. So the real question becomes: Are you shrinking to fit someone else's version of "acceptable"? Or are you standing tall in your own truth and authenticity?

**You don't owe anyone**
**a muted version of yourself.**

Start noticing where you dim your light.
And then—*flip the switch back on.*

# Building the Skill: Embodying Your Vivacious Energy

Vivaciousness isn't just a personality trait—it's a practice. It's something you can nurture and expand by being intentional about how you show up and recharge. These strategies will help you cultivate a life filled with energy, joy, and vibrant presence.

1. **Tap into your joy triggers.**
   What makes you feel most alive? Dancing, singing, storytelling, and connecting with others? Schedule time for those things—not as a luxury but as a necessity.
2. **Practice radiant presence.**
   When you walk into a room, do it with intention—do it with purpose. Smile. Make eye contact. Radiate warmth. People feel energy—let them feel yours.
3. **Laugh out loud.**
   Really. Let yourself belly-laugh more often. Playfulness is a muscle, and the more you engage with it, the more it shows up naturally.
4. **Own your expression.**
   Whether it's a bold outfit, a quirky sense of humor, or animated storytelling, give yourself full permission to show up as the vibrant woman you are.
5. **Be the spark for others.**
   Use your vivaciousness to uplift the people around you. Compliment freely, encourage often, and let your energy be a ripple of joy.

I've lived these practices. I've lost my spark and worked to get it back. Vivaciousness isn't about being "on" all the time—it's about showing up with joy, energy, and authenticity when you can, and being kind to yourself when you can't. Today, I live louder, laugh more freely, and bring that same vibrant energy to those around me.

You can, too.

*Your vivaciousness is a gift—and it's one the world needs.*

## Final Roar

Your light is not a liability—it's your superpower.
When you lead with joy, you give others permission to rise.
So keep showing up. Keep laughing out loud. Keep shaking those pom poms.
Even when your flame dims, know this: ***The spark is still there***.
And it only takes a moment of truth, a breath of kindness,
or a shift in purpose to reignite it.
Be bold. Be bright. Be vivacious.
***Because the world needs your fire.***

# Passionate

## What It Means to Be Passionate

The word passion comes from the Latin *passio*, meaning "to suffer" or "to endure." But in our modern context, passion isn't just about suffering—it's about caring so deeply about something that you're willing to give your time, energy, and heart to it. And that level of commitment can take on a very different form depending on the setting. This deep-rooted commitment empowers us, fuels our leadership, and gives us the confidence to make a lasting impact.

I am often told that I'm passionate about my work. It's true. I show up with enthusiasm, drive, and a deep desire to lead effectively, deliver results, and ensure my team operates with integrity and excellence. But here's the thing—"passionate" is not always used like it's a compliment.

There have been many times in my life when my energy has been labeled "too intense." I've been told to scale it back, dial down my passion for the sake of comfort, ease up, slow down, back up, you name it, I've probably heard it. But I've learned something in my many years of experience: when someone asks you to tone it down, it often says more about *their discomfort, insecurity, and lack of confidence* than it does about your delivery.

One of the clearest examples of passion came very early in my career. I was working on a massive project that had been drastically undersold. The scope was enormous, the timeline stretched to over a year, and the resources we were given fell short of what we needed. I poured everything into that project—my time, my energy, my weekends, my heart.

But the moment I remember most wasn't about the outcome of the project. It was when I had to sit across from my boss—and later, his boss—and push for something they didn't want to hear. I told them the truth: we needed more resources. Yes, it would hurt our bottom line. But the alternative was cutting corners, skimping on the quality and even quantity of the deliverables for the client, and I wouldn't let that happen. I knew the project had been low-balled by sales. I knew it wasn't fair. But fairness didn't matter to me as much as doing the right thing.

I wasn't popular for it. I got a lot of pushback. I was even told I didn't have enough experience to know what I was talking about or the impact of what I was suggesting. But I didn't care. Passion doesn't care about popularity. It cares about principles. And that day, I stood firm—not because it was easy, but because my integrity demanded it. Passion fueled that decision. And I'd make the same decision again.

Let's confront a societal bias head-on—the same passion that garners applause in men is often labeled as emotional in women. A man speaks with fervor, and he's seen as strong and speaking with conviction. A woman does the same, and she's seen as "too intense" or "taking things personally." The playing field isn't level, but we *can* shift how we show up and challenge those narratives, with awareness and intention.

That starts with self-awareness. If I notice that my passion might be overwhelming someone—or if the room feels like it's shutting down—I pause. I ask questions. I invite others into the dialogue: "What are your thoughts?" or "What am I missing from your perspective?" It's not about dimming my light; it's about making space for others to shine too. It's about diverting that passion into efforts that create inclusion for others in the conversation.

Passion doesn't always have to be loud. Some of the most powerful passion comes through a calm, deliberate voice. Quiet passion can be even more compelling when grounded in expertise and conviction. Stick to the facts. Remove unnecessary emotion. And own your authority on the subject.

Being passionate doesn't mean being inflexible, either. True passion includes humility—the willingness to listen, evolve, and admit when someone else brings a valuable insight you hadn't considered. That's not weakness. That's strength.

## Are You Holding Yourself Back?

Have you ever quieted your voice to make others more comfortable? Have you ever second-guessed your enthusiasm, worried it might be "excessive"? If so, you're not alone.

Women are often conditioned—directly or indirectly—to dial back their passion. We're told not to come on too strong. To be "likeable." To not rock the boat. In doing so, we often suppress the very thing that makes us great.

*Passion is not a flaw to fix—*
*it's a force to own.*

Sometimes, we hold ourselves back because of fear: fear of judgment, fear of rejection, fear of appearing "emotional" or "irrational." But here's the truth—when channeled with clarity and purpose, passion is one of the most powerful leadership traits you can possess.

*The problem isn't that you're too passionate.*
*The problem is that others*
*may not know how to receive your fire.*

That is their work to do, not yours to internalize. Ask yourself:

- Do I hold back in meetings even when I feel strongly about an idea?
- Do I soften my voice or words so I don't seem "pushy"?
- Do I question my value when others don't match my energy?

It's time to shift the mindset. Your passion is not just allowed—it's essential. The world needs your fire, your spark, your voice. Let it rise.

# Build the Skill: Strategies to Embody Passionate Leadership

You don't have to quell your fire—you just have to learn how to channel it. Passion, when directed with clarity and intention, becomes a leadership superpower. The following strategies will help you harness your enthusiasm in ways that inspire, connect, and create lasting impact.

1. **Know the difference between passion and emotion.**
   Passion is grounded in purpose. *It's your why.* Emotion, while valid, can sometimes cloud your delivery. Practice presenting your passion through facts, results, and personal experience—rooted in calm confidence. Let your passion lead, not overwhelm.

2. **Read the room—then invite it in.**
   Passion doesn't exist in a vacuum. Pay attention to how your energy is being received. If you sense hesitation, don't retreat. Instead, invite others in: "What's your take?" or "How do you see it differently?" This creates a connection without compromising your presence.

3. **Don't apologize for caring deeply.**
   Stop prefacing your ideas with "Sorry, but..." or "I just think..." Your passion doesn't require an apology. Say what you mean. Say it clearly. And trust that your passion will bring value to the conversation. (*Anyone who knows me personally: you know this is one of my biggest personal challenges!*)

4. **Reclaim the narrative.**
   If someone labels you as "too much," flip the script. Say, "I'm passionate about this because I care deeply about the outcome." Reframing helps shift the perception from emotional to intentional.

5. **Recharge your fire.**
   Even the most passionate people burn out. Schedule regular time to reconnect with what fuels you—journaling, music, creative projects, movement, community, or something else. Passion needs refueling to stay lit.

6. **Celebrate passion in others.**

   Model what it looks like to receive someone else's passion with encouragement rather than discomfort. When you amplify the passion of others, you normalize it in your environment.

Through both challenge and clarity, I've learned that passion isn't something to control. It's something to cultivate.

> *When used with intention,*
> *passion becomes the driving force*
> *behind authentic leadership,*
> *courageous communication,*
> *and lasting change.*

You don't have to hold it back. You just have to let it burn in the right direction.

## Final Roar

Your passion is your power. Not everyone will know what to do with your fire—ignite anyway.

Some may ask you to shrink—stand taller.

Some may call you emotional—let them.

You're not here to be palatable. You're here to lead.

Be bold. Be blazing. Be passionate.

Because the world doesn't need you to be quiet.

*It needs you to be on fire.*

# ROAR LIKE A WOMAN

# Effortless

## What It Means to Be Effortless

There's a certain magic in watching someone do something with such ease that it feels like breathing—fluid, graceful, second nature. We often call it effortless. But what we don't see is the truth underneath: effortless doesn't mean easy. It means earned.

For me, effortless has nothing to do with the absence of effort. It's what happens after you've done the deep work—after the late nights, the internal battles, the thousand tiny choices to stay grounded instead of reactive. It's the product of preparation, intention, and emotional discipline. You've done the reps. You've trained your mind. You've shaped your energy.

Most of my career has been spent in fast-paced, high-pressure environments—project launches, production escalations, and constant fires that demand immediate attention. The chaos can feel endless. But at some point, I stopped bracing for impact and started preparing for it. I developed habits that strengthened my resilience, learned how to regulate my emotions, and trained myself to respond rather than react. The result? I can walk into a storm and stay calm. Do I always succeed? No. Do I usually recognize the reactions and try to course-correct? Yes. That's when people started to say, "You make it look easy." And I would smile because I knew it only looked that way.

But it wasn't always like that. I recall a project where I led a high-stakes integration across multiple departments. The deadlines were aggressive, the leadership expectations sky-high, and every decision felt like it could break something—budget, timeline, or people. I was in meetings back-to-back, answering late-night emails, and putting out fires before I could even sip my coffee. On the outside, I looked calm, composed, and in control. People would say, "You're so poised. How do you do it all so effortlessly?"

But what they didn't see was the journal entries, where I poured out my anxiety. The deep breaths I took before walking into a room. Or the way I would look in the mirror before work and hype myself up like a coach before a championship game. *Don't let the chaos distract you. Go slay the day and show them who is queen.* I needed those affirmations just to step out the door with intention.

That version of me didn't feel effortless—I felt stretched thin. But I showed up anyway. And through it all, I discovered something: I didn't have to eliminate the chaos to remain calm. I just had to anchor myself deeper. That's when effortlessness stopped being a performance and began to become a practice.

Effortless is not about perfection or pretending. It's about being so rooted in yourself that external noise doesn't shake you. It's about showing up with grace, even when your world feels like a tornado. Effortless women are not without struggle—they've just made peace with it.

So many fierce women in our society embody this effortless strength. Michelle Obama is one of the first to come to mind. Thrust into a global spotlight where every move, every word, and every outfit was scrutinized, she remained poised, intelligent, classy, and deeply human. Her speeches, her presence, and even her style feel natural and fluid because they're grounded in authenticity and preparation. She exudes effortless power.

Other strong women, like Oprah Winfrey, Maya Angelou (legacy), and Mel Robbins, also carry this same energy. They've walked through fire, done the work, and cultivated presence, patience, and self-mastery over years of learning and healing. Now, what we see is the outcome: leadership that feels effortless.

What all of these women share is more than poise—it's a legacy. Their ease and presence weren't inherited without effort; they were forged through generations of wisdom, struggle, and strength. They remind me that we don't carry this journey alone. We move forward with the whispers of the women before us in our ears, with their resilience in our bones. Effortless power is never just personal—it's ancestral.

> *"For me, becoming isn't about arriving somewhere or*
> *achieving a certain aim.*
> *I see it instead as forward motion,*
> *a means of evolving,*
> *a way to reach continuously toward a better self.*
> *The journey doesn't end."*
> — Michelle Obama, *Becoming*

That quote from Michelle Obama's memoir resonates deeply with me. I'm constantly evolving. Every new experience and lesson learned brings me closer to the version of myself I want to be—one who leads with confidence and exudes a sense of ease in the face of complexity. That's what effortless means to me.

## Are You Holding Yourself Back?

Even when we admire effortlessness in others, we don't always believe it's possible for ourselves. We've been taught that ease must be earned through exhaustion, but that belief may be the very thing holding us back.

Let's explore some beliefs that might be blocking your ability to experience true effortless ease:

- Do you equate success with constant struggle or burnout, and feel guilty when things flow easily?
- Are you addicted to over-performing, thinking that being "busy" is the same as being valuable?
- Do you fear being judged if things appear too easy for you, so you overcompensate by working harder than necessary?

- Have you neglected the inner work, thinking that only the external hustle matters?
- Do you struggle with letting go of control, believing it won't get done right if you don't do it all yourself?
- Do you downplay your ease or grace to make others more comfortable?

If any of these resonate with you, you're not alone. Many of us are conditioned to believe that ease is laziness, that grace is weakness, and that being soft makes us less strong. But what if the opposite is true? What if effortlessness is the ultimate display of inner strength?

## Building the Skill: Embracing Effortless Power

To embody effortless power, we must begin with intention. It's not about doing less—it's about doing what matters with a sense of calm, clarity, and confidence. True effortlessness is built over time, through consistency, emotional maturity, and a deep trust in your own rhythm. Here are a few ways to get started:

1. **Prepare to perform.**
   Effortless doesn't mean unprepared—it means so prepared that your response becomes second nature. Rehearse. Reflect. Revisit your goals.
2. **Master your mindset.**
   Start your day with affirmations like "I am grounded," "I move with ease," and "I trust myself." These create a baseline of calm that carries over into how you present yourself.
3. **Simplify your environment.**
   Remove the unnecessary. Streamline your tasks, delegate where possible, and create space for flow.
4. **Practice emotional regulation.**
   Learn to pause before reacting. Clear your head with breathwork, journaling, or a walk. Respond with focus instead of reacting with chaos.

5. **Trust your preparation.**
   You've done the work. Let yourself step into the moment with grace and assurance. You don't need to prove—you need to be.

6. **Let go of perfection.**
   Effortlessness is not about flawlessness. It's about fluidity. Grace. Forward motion.

7. **Be fully present.**
   Effortless energy flows when you're here, not in your head. Release the need to control every outcome. Make eye contact. Listen deeply. Let your presence speak louder than your performance.

*When you align your preparation with presence,*
*effortlessness stops being a performance*
*and starts being who you are.*

## Final Roar

Maya Angelou once said, *"I come as one, but I stand as ten thousand."*

That quote gives me chills every time I hear it.

Because that is the root of effortless power.

It's not about walking alone or pretending you don't feel fear. It's about knowing that every step you take is grounded in something deeper. Something ancient. Something that comes from within you—but also from every experience, lesson, and woman who came before you.

When I show up as effortless, I'm not hiding the work. I'm honoring it. I'm moving with intention, not panic. I'm standing not just on my own strength—but on the shoulders of generations.

Effortless doesn't mean you didn't sweat, cry, or fight to get here. It means you made peace with the process. You've accepted the flow. You've stopped gripping the wheel so tightly that it breaks. It's about accepting yourself, flaws and all, and still showing up with grace and confidence.

You've become the kind of woman who can step into chaos and steady the room with her presence. Who commands respect not through volume, but through calm certainty. Who leads with grace—and make no mistake, that grace was forged through fire.

*Effortless is earned.*
*And you've earned it too.*

# Radiant

## What It Means to Be Radiant

The word radiant stems from the Latin root *radiāre*, meaning "to shine, to beam, to emit rays of light." And that's exactly how I want to live: beaming with light and glowing from the inside out. But being radiant isn't about surface-level beauty or being the loudest person in the room. For me, radiance is a quiet but unmistakable force—it's the energy I choose to carry into the world every single day.

Recently, I made a profound commitment to myself. Every morning, I wake up an hour earlier than I used to. As someone who's never been a morning person, that extra hour means a lot. I devote that sacred time to writing what Julia Cameron calls *Morning Pages*—three pages of uncensored, stream-of-consciousness writing intended to clear mental clutter and spark creativity. I also use this time to write affirmations and manifestations, not just once but repeatedly. These are not mere motivational quotes—they're the messages I want imprinted on my heart.

*I am proud of who I am becoming each day.*

*I let go of what I cannot control and focus on what I can.*

*I am a beacon of light spreading positivity wherever I go.*

By the time I finish writing, I've already set the tone of my day—and that tone is light.

Since committing to this morning ritual, something extraordinary has happened. People have noticed. Co-workers, friends—even casual acquaintances—have stopped me in the hallway or during meetings to say, "You look so happy," or "There's something about your energy—it's magnetic." One person even said, "Your face is radiating happiness." That one stuck with me. I had never thought of myself as radiant, but hearing it out loud made me realize: this is what radiance truly is. It's not about how I look—but what I emit. And what I'm emitting now is joy, calm, and intention.

But I haven't always felt this way. There have been times in my life—especially during high-stress seasons—when pressure, disappointment, and burnout weighed me down so much that I allowed my light to be completely dimmed. I was showing up to life, but I wasn't shining. I was surviving, not thriving. That inner glow was buried beneath the chaos.

And then something shifted.

In May of 2025, I traveled to the Dominican Republic to attend a destination wedding for two dear friends, Ryan and Kristin. I felt honored to be included in their intimate circle of friends and family, and even then, I sensed that this trip would be important for me. What I didn't know was just how important. I had committed to the trip months earlier, but it wasn't until I arrived—surrounded by sunshine, sand, ocean, and tropical beauty—that I realized how much I had been carrying. It was as if, during that week, I finally exhaled. I released months—maybe years—of built-up tension, stress, frustration, and inner restlessness.

One afternoon, I was sitting alone on the beach, enjoying the calm and soothing sounds of the waves, birds, and rustling palm leaves. And then, a shift happened that I hadn't expected. Something broke open inside me. Without warning, I broke down sobbing uncontrollably.

I sat there for almost thirty minutes, releasing everything I hadn't even realized I was holding. In that stillness, something broke open. I realized that what I had been searching for—my reason, my spark, my truth—had been right in front of me all along.

I found my true purpose that day. Through that spiritual awakening, I understood that my joy, my calling, my superpower is in helping others recognize and value their own worth. I want to help others discover their *vibrant potential*, especially when they can't see it for themselves yet.

That trip reignited the creative spark that had been quietly flickering in the background of my soul. It broke through my writer's block and ultimately gave me the momentum to finish this book. You're reading it now because of what was unlocked in me that week.

And when I returned home, people noticed again—but this time, it wasn't just about energy. It was about presence. I was glowing. Truly glowing. My smile came more easily, my eyes sparkled, and my voice carried more warmth. There was a new lightness in my step and a beautiful joy in my heart. I was radiant—not because life was suddenly perfect, but because I had realigned with what brings me happiness and fulfillment. I had remembered who I am and what I'm here to do.

**I had reclaimed my purpose.**

I've come to understand this: radiance is not something you're born with—it's something you choose and cultivate. It's born in the quiet moments, in the intentional pauses, and in the decisions to guard your peace and protect your energy. I believe that my commitment to optimism, creativity, and meaningful connection is what makes me radiant.

And that glow? It's contagious. I never considered myself radiant, but I now understand that radiance is only one of many traits that empower us to ignite passion in others. Are you ready to cultivate your inner glow?

*"Be a rainbow in someone else's cloud."*
— Maya Angelou

## Are You Holding Yourself Back?

It's easy to think of radiance as something reserved for "other people"—the effortlessly joyful, the outwardly attractive, the natural-born extroverts. But the truth is, radiance isn't about any of that. It's not a physical trait. It's not something you buy. It's not even about how loud or bubbly you are. Radiance is an inner glow that comes from how you choose to engage with the world.

So ask yourself:

- Do I start my day with intention, or do I jump into chaos?
- Do I allow the negativity of others to dim my spirit?
- Do I complain more than I celebrate?
- Am I waiting for something external to make me happy before I permit myself to shine?

You might be holding yourself back from radiance without even realizing it. Sometimes, we dim our light because we fear standing out or don't want to make others uncomfortable. Sometimes, we've learned that being "too positive" is naïve or unrealistic. But here's the truth: positivity is a courageous choice. It's a radical act of resilience in a world that often thrives on cynicism.

You are allowed to glow. You are allowed to beam. You are allowed to radiate joy, even when the world feels messy. You don't need permission from anyone else to shine.

The only permission you need is your own.

## Building the Skill: How to Cultivate Radiance

If you want to build a more radiant life and presence, it starts with small, intentional habits that fuel your inner light. Radiance is something you cultivate. Here are strategies that can help you glow—inside and out:

1. **Begin your day with morning pages.**
   Try setting aside 30–45 minutes each morning to write freely. Buy a fancy notebook or journal to write in that brings you joy. Let your thoughts pour onto the pages without editing or censoring. This practice clears mental clutter, making space for clarity, creativity, and calm.
2. **Anchor your day with affirmations.**
   Write three to five affirmations that speak to your power and joy. Here are some examples to get those affirmative vibes flowing: "I radiate

light and positivity." "I am a source of peace." "I choose to be positive despite negativity." "My energy uplifts others." Repeat them aloud or in writing daily.

3. **Choose your circle with care.**

Pay attention to the energy of the people around you. If specific environments drain you or pull you into negativity, create healthy boundaries. Protect your glow.

4. **Detox from toxicity.**

This includes conversations, media, and even your own thoughts. When you catch yourself spiraling into doom and gloom, pause. Reframe. Look for the lesson to be learned or the light in the situation.

5. **Smile more, laugh often.**

Genuine laughter and joyful expression are powerful radiators of energy. Find things that make you laugh and make time for them. Joy is contagious.

6. **Rest and nourish yourself.**

Radiance doesn't come from burnout. Prioritize rest, hydration, and foods that make you feel good. You shine brightest when you're replenished.

7. **Practice presence.**

Radiance grows in the present moment. The more you live in the now— fully aware, fully engaged—the more grounded and glowing you'll become.

8. **Lead with light.**

Make it your mission to bring light to others. A kind word, a warm gesture, or simply being fully present with someone can change their day—and yours.

I have tried many of the above strategies myself, and I can attest that I now have a more positive outlook on life. I experience joy in my heart, and know that I am radiant—and it's contagious. I want you to find that radiance within yourself, too.

It's already there, waiting to be uncovered.

## Final Roar

Radiance isn't something you chase—it's something you choose.

It's a daily decision to shine, no matter the weather.

You have the power to glow from the inside out, and this world needs your light.

Let them feel your joy.

Let them see your spark.

Let them be moved by your presence.

*You are radiant.*
*And the world is brighter because of it.*

# Charismatic

## What It Means to Be Charismatic

You know when someone walks into a room and the energy shifts—subtly, but unmistakably? Not because they're loud or flashy, but because they're *fully present.* That's charisma.

When I think of someone who embodies that kind of presence, Oprah Winfrey comes to mind immediately. I imagine the room softens and sharpens all at once when she enters—not from ego, but from energy. Her presence radiates humility, grace, calm authority, and deep authenticity. That's the kind of energy I aspire to bring into every space I enter.

To me, charisma isn't about being the most outgoing person in the room. It's not about charm or polish. It's about being a source of *positive movement*—someone who can walk into a space and breathe life back into it. I want to be the kind of leader who reignites a discouraged team, asks the hard question in a quiet room, or simply steadies the energy when things start to unravel.

Charisma and charm often get lumped together, but they're not the same thing. I've known plenty of charming people—many of them quite lovely—but sometimes that charm can also feel performative or even a little manipulative. It draws people in, sometimes with an agenda, relying on surface-level appeal or polished façades to win favor. Charm can be fleeting—a tool to impress or persuade—but it doesn't always foster genuine connection or trust.

Charisma, on the other hand, is genuine. It comes without ulterior motives. It doesn't seek to outshine others—it aims to uplift. A charismatic person doesn't work the room for themselves; they work it for the room. Their goal is to elevate, energize, and unite.

I think about my parents—two of the most quietly charismatic people I've ever known. They didn't chase titles or seek the spotlight, but people gravitated toward them anyway. Our home was always full—of laughter, of stories, of people who felt safe there. I watched my parents listen with their whole hearts, greet others with warmth, and show up again and again with presence and patience, especially when someone was hurting.

They were deeply spiritual people, and their faith wasn't something they used to exclude others—it was something they used to *connect*. Over the years, they helped start small community churches not for recognition, but to create spaces of love, belonging, and outreach.

What I remember most, though, were the conversations around our dinner table. My parents were endlessly curious about people from other walks of life. They welcomed interfaith dialogue with such openness—talking with guests about different religions, exploring similarities and differences, and always circling back to a simple truth: we are more alike than we are different. They didn't need big speeches or grand gestures to influence people. Their steady energy, their deep care, their genuine interest in others—that was their charisma.

And that's the heart of it. Charisma isn't about being bold for boldness's sake. It's about creating space. Shifting the room. Choosing presence over perfection.

I've had my own moments when that presence faltered—times I've been reactive, flustered, or shut down. But those moments taught me that charisma isn't about flawless composure. It's about emotional awareness. The most charismatic leaders I know aren't the ones who dominate—they're the ones who *listen*, reset, and lead with intention.

At its core, charisma is *influence with integrity*. It's courage paired with connection. It's the power to shift energy—for the better—just by showing up as the most grounded, authentic version of yourself.

## Are You Holding Yourself Back?

Charisma often gets misunderstood. Many people assume you must be loud, extroverted, or "naturally" magnetic to be charismatic, but that's not true. At its core, charisma is about how you make people feel. It's about presence, intentionality, and connection. And you don't have to be the life of the party to have it.

You may be holding yourself back from stepping into your charismatic power if:

- You dim your light to avoid being seen as "too much."
- You stay silent in meetings even when you know your input could benefit the group.
- You feel nervous advocating for others because you fear standing out.
- You think charisma is something you're either born with or not.
- You don't think you have what it takes to be charismatic.

But charisma can be developed. It's a skill, not just a trait. One of the most empowering ways to embrace your charisma is by showing up fully—for yourself and for others. It's about being courageous enough to speak when it matters, to genuinely connect with people, and to energize a space with your authenticity.

## Building the Skill: Strategies to Cultivate Charisma

Charisma isn't just something you have—it's something you build. With intention and daily practice, you can become someone who lights up a room, influences with heart, and leads with presence.

Here are some ways to cultivate that energy:

1. **Start with intentional energy.**
   Before stepping into any space—whether it's a meeting, a conversation, or a crowded room—pause and ask yourself: "What kind of energy do I

want to bring?" Uplifting? Grounding? Inspiring? Let that intention shape your presence, posture, and how your words land.

2. **Listen deeply and make people feel heard.**

Charismatic people often say less and listen more. Practice active listening—make eye contact, nod, ask clarifying questions, and reflect back what you hear. People gravitate toward those who make them feel seen.

3. **Use your voice with courage.**

Speak up when it counts—for yourself and others. Charisma grows when you advocate compassionately and confidently, especially when others are hesitant or afraid to do so. It's not just about your own voice, but about using it to amplify the voices of others.

4. **Stay grounded and emotionally attuned.**

Emotional presence is key. When you're centered and self-aware, you can navigate tension, shift dynamics, and calm the chaos. People remember how you made them feel—be the calm in the storm.

5. **Own your unique presence.**

Charisma doesn't come from imitation. It comes from being fully, unapologetically yourself. Whether your style is bold or understated, what matters is that it's genuine. Your authenticity is your power.

6. **Use eye contact and a warm smile to connect.**

These small gestures go a long way. They show you're present, approachable, and open—the foundation of every meaningful connection.

Charisma is not performance—it's presence. It's not about stealing the spotlight, but about sharing your soul. The more you lead with empathy, energy, and authenticity, the more your charisma shines—not as something you *manufacture*, but as something you *live*.

You don't need to change who you are.

You need to let who you are come through.

# Final Roar

Charisma is the quiet courage to lead with integrity, to energize with empathy, and to inspire through action.

You don't need a spotlight to be charismatic—you just need the confidence to be fully, authentically you.

If you've ever spoken up for someone else, helped a group feel seen, or shifted the mood in a meeting with your energy—you've already stepped into the power of charisma.

The world needs more of that.

The world needs more of *you*.

*Charisma isn't about being*
*the loudest voice in the room—*
*it's about showing up*
*with presence, purpose, and heart.*

# III

# Rise Up

# Strength, Grit, and Resilience

This part of your journey is about power—the kind that's built, not given. The kind you earn with every climb, every scar, every time you've stood back up and said: "Not today."

These next chapters focus on the strength it takes to rise up after setbacks, to hold your ground, and to push forward even when the odds are stacked against you. In Part III, words like *Tenacious*, *Resilient*, *Grit*, and *Unstoppable* will meet you where you are—and call forth the fire that refuses to quit.

We often think of strength as loud or forceful, but true resilience is quietly forged in the fires of daily choices, difficult moments, and unseen battles. It's in the decision to keep showing up. In the way you face fear and uncertainty with a steady heart. In your refusal to back down from what matters most.

This is your power. Your control. Your resilience.

We are often told to be soft. To be small. To smile more. To take up less space. But let's not forget: we are also forged from steel and shine with the strength of a diamond. We are the backbone of movements, the lifeblood of families, the voice of change. We are both tenderness and tenacity. And we are at our strongest when we recognize that vulnerability and grit are not opposites—they are partners.

This section isn't just about pushing through. It's about *rising up*—on your own terms, in your own time, and always #WithPurpose. It's about knowing when to dig deep, when to rest, and when to roar. It's about remembering that every action and every decision is driven by something deeper: a truth you carry, a goal you are shaping, a future you are claiming.

Let these words remind you that you are unbreakable. That you can be soft and fierce. Gentle and powerful. And every time you rise, you inspire someone else to believe they can too.

So breathe. Rise. And let's roar together.

# Bold

## What It Means to Be Bold

Boldness isn't always loud. Sometimes it's the quietest person in the room refusing to look away.

Sometimes, it's a woman in her twenties, walking into a male-dominated tech lab and deciding, day after day, that she won't shrink to fit in.

And that was me.

Early in my career, I was one of only a handful of women in technical roles working on our project team. Most of the other women on our floor were in administrative roles, and the lab—where the real technical work happened—was locked down and filled almost entirely with men. When I finally earned a spot inside that technical lab circle, I was proud of it... until I saw what was on the walls.

Pin-up calendars. Crude humor. Locker-room energy masked as culture.

I didn't raise my voice or make a formal complaint. I simply started removing the calendars—folding them up and placing them neatly in desk drawers. Every day. For weeks. It became a quiet routine... and, for a while, a subtle power struggle. But over time, something shifted. The jokes slowed. The posters disappeared for good. And the same men who once rolled their eyes began to listen when I spoke.

That was one of my first lessons in boldness. It wasn't about spectacle. It was about principle.

Boldness, I realized, could look like steady resistance. Quiet courage.

Boundaries drawn with grace.

The word *bold* comes from the Old English *beald* and the Latin *audax*—meaning "daring, brave, and courageous." But in today's world, especially for women, boldness is still too often misinterpreted. It's labeled as difficult. Aggressive. Unlikable. But here's the truth: boldness isn't about ego. It's about *integrity*. It's the decision to show up fully, speak truth when it's inconvenient, and lead from a place of clarity and conviction.

Today, I live and lead by a mantra: **Act on everything #WithPurpose.** It's more than a hashtag—it's a compass. I want everything I do to be driven by intention and anchored in integrity. So when I speak hard truths—about budgets, people, and priorities—I do so with the goal of solving, not shaming. Of moving things forward, not blowing things up.

As women, we're often walking a tightrope. Speak too softly, and we're dismissed. Speak too boldly, and we're labeled aggressive or difficult. I've spent years learning how to walk that line with grace. I lean into facts. I choose calm language. I drop qualifiers like "I think" or "maybe." And yes, I still catch myself softening the truth with a disclaimer like, "I'm sorry, but..."

*Boldness has taught me this:*
*truth doesn't need an apology.*

It's taken practice. I've had moments when boldness left me feeling exposed, vulnerable, and misunderstood. There were times when speaking up meant being left out. There were moments when my boldness cost me approval or made others uncomfortable. And yet, I've never regretted telling the truth.

I've learned that speaking the truth—especially when it's awkward—is not just bold. It's essential.

That's how trust is built. That's how respect is earned.

And that's how change begins.

## Are You Holding Yourself Back?

Boldness doesn't always look like a grand gesture or a headline-making move. Sometimes, it's the quiet decision to raise your hand, send the email, or tell the truth in a room full of silence. And yet, boldness can be the very thing we talk ourselves out of—especially when we've been conditioned to prioritize politeness over honesty, or harmony over impact.

If you struggle to speak up or step forward, you're not alone. But it's worth asking yourself—*why am I hesitating?*

- Do you hesitate to share your perspective because you fear how others will react?
- Do you soften your language with apologies or disclaimers, even when you're right?
- Are you waiting for someone else to speak the truth first so you don't have to?

Being bold doesn't mean being reckless. It means you value the truth more than the comfort of silence. If you're holding back from saying what needs to be said because you're afraid of being judged or labeled, ask yourself this: *What happens if no one else speaks up?*

The moment you decide to share your truth clearly, concisely, and unapologetically—that's where your power lies. Let boldness become your signal of integrity, not your source of shame.

## Building the Skill: How to Embrace Boldness

Boldness is not just a trait. It's a skill that can be developed. You don't wake up one day suddenly fearless—it's something you build through repetition, self-awareness, and choosing truth over comfort. The more you speak with conviction, the more natural it becomes. The following strategies will help you sharpen your boldness while staying grounded in your values.

1. **Replace apologies with facts.**

   The next time you catch yourself starting with "I'm sorry, but..." pause. Reframe it with factual language: "Here's the current situation, and here's how we're addressing it." Leading with facts shows confidence and credibility.

2. **Anchor your voice in purpose.**

   Before a challenging conversation or meeting, revisit your core values or your personal mantra. This will remind you that your intention is grounded, not aggressive. Purpose gives your message weight without needing volume.

3. **Practice bold delivery.**

   Rehearse difficult messages out loud. Pay attention to your tone and body language. Boldness isn't just in what you say—it's in how you say it. Calm clarity often makes the biggest impact.

4. **Challenge the status quo—out loud.**

   Boldness means being willing to say what others are thinking but afraid to voice. When you see something that feels misaligned—whether it's a broken process, an outdated mindset, or an unspoken double standard—name it. Ask the question no one else wants to ask. Not to stir the pot, but to clear the air. True change always begins with discomfort.

5. **Eliminate qualifiers.**

   Avoid phrases like "I think," "I could be wrong," or "maybe." Replace them with stronger statements: "The data shows...," "We've assessed the risk...," or "This is the impact." Strong language reflects strong leadership.

6. **Build credibility over time.**

   Boldness becomes more powerful when backed by a track record of integrity and results. When you consistently deliver truth with respect, people trust your voice, even when the message is hard to hear.

7. **Be willing to be misunderstood.**

If you're always perfectly understood, you're probably not saying anything new. Boldness comes with risk—and that includes the risk of being misinterpreted, judged, or even disliked. But growth doesn't happen in the safe zone. Trust that clarity will catch up to courage. Don't shrink your truth to make it more palatable.

> *Boldness isn't about being fearless—*
> *it's about acting despite fear.*

The more you practice speaking with intention and clarity, the more natural it becomes. Your bold voice might not be the loudest in the room, but it will always be heard when it comes from a place of truth and integrity.

## Final Roar

Boldness doesn't require a spotlight. It doesn't always come with applause. Sometimes, being bold means telling the truth when it's inconvenient. Speaking up when others stay silent. Choosing purpose over popularity.

You don't have to shout to be bold—but you have to stand tall in your truth. Whenever you speak with clarity, lead with integrity, and act with intention, you choose a path that honors who you are. You're showing the world that boldness is not about ego—it's about courage.

I will speak with clarity.

I will act with intention.

I will lead with the truth.

**I will be bold on purpose.**

# Grit

## What It Means to Have Grit

My first meaningful encounter with the concept of grit was through a workplace book club. We were reading *Grit* by Angela Duckworth, and as I absorbed her research and insights, something inside me clicked. It was as if she were describing me. I realized—I am this word. Grit isn't just a motivational buzzword. It's a way of being. It's a part of who I am.

By definition, grit is a personality trait characterized by passion and perseverance in pursuit of long-term goals. If that doesn't describe how I approach life, then I don't know what does. Of course, I'm not perfect. I don't always hit every goal. But I live with determination, and I show up again and again. That's grit.

When I think about the traits that define someone with true grit—*resilience, persistence, discipline, courage,* and *hard work*—I see myself striving toward those traits every single day. I haven't lived the most difficult life, but I've had my share of tough times. And when those challenging moments come, I always seem to find a way to push through. Not because I have all the answers, but because I refuse to give up.

One of the most defining moments of grit in my life came in my early 40s. I was in a relationship with someone who already had a child on the way from a prior relationship. Shortly after we began our life together, his daughter was born. Over time, I became more than a partner—I became a mother, not by biology, but by every other measure. I fed her, held her when she cried, helped her with school projects, and loved her unconditionally. She was mine. And when she finally called me "mom" of her own accord, it was a title I never took for granted.

However, life doesn't always honor the depth of love with the same weight that it honors legality. When my relationship with her father ended—and it ended painfully—I faced a devastating reality: I had no legal rights to the now 10-year-old child I had raised. None. But I couldn't just walk away. That's not who I am.

At the time, her father, who held full legal custody, filed a petition with the court, requesting permission from her biological mother to move the child I had raised out of state. If the petition were approved, it would mean losing daily connection with the child I had poured a decade of love and life into. I wasn't listed in the documents. I had no voice in the decision. But I knew I couldn't stay silent.

So I did what grit required. I hired a lawyer. I attempted to join the custody case as a third-party guardian, not to spite anyone but to protect the child I loved. I was ready to fight for her, to adopt her, and to continue being her mother. I knew the system wasn't designed to support someone in my position, but I had to try—for her.

In the end, the courts denied my request—because of a technicality, no less. A filing was one day late. One day. That single day changed the course of both of our lives. She moved out of state with her father, and I was left grieving a child who was still very much alive. For years, he controlled when—and if—I could have contact with her. A phone call here, a brief visit there. I was no longer allowed to be called "Mom." I was recast as a nanny. He stripped away the role I had lovingly played for a decade, reducing our bond to something transactional. From age ten to eighteen, I lived in a kind of emotional limbo—waiting, hoping, and loving from a distance.

But that's not the end of the story.

Because grit doesn't give up. Grit keeps loving. Grit keeps believing. And when my daughter turned eighteen, and was legally an adult, she *found me*. We *reconnected*. We cried.

**And today, she is still *my daughter*.**

That bond—built not by blood but by heart—is unbreakable.

Time has a way of revealing what truly matters. And in the end, love rooted in truth, presence, and unwavering care will always rise. Some things can't be taken away—not by law, not by distance, and not by anyone who didn't understand the power of a mother's love.

What fuels that inner fire to keep going? I don't think there's a one-size-fits-all answer. If there were, I'd bottle it and become a billionaire! But I do know this:

> **Grit begins when you**
> **acknowledge that you're struggling—**
> **and decide that you're**
> **not going to stay stuck there.**

It's not about pretending everything is fine. It's about being honest, finding your footing, and taking one step forward.

For me, that often means talking it out or writing through the pain. And sometimes, it means asking for help. *That's part of grit, too—knowing you don't have to do it all alone.* Whether it's friends, family, a therapist, or a hotline, help is always available (see *You Are Not Alone* at the back of the book for a list of national hotlines and mental health resources). You are never weak for reaching out. In fact, asking for support may be the most courageous thing you ever do.

## Are You Holding Yourself Back?

This section invites honest self-reflection. Grit isn't reserved for the strongest or loudest—it's something we can all cultivate when we pause and examine the stories we tell ourselves.

- Are you giving up on yourself too soon when things get hard?
- Do you tell yourself that discipline and resilience just aren't part of your nature?

- Are you afraid to ask for help because it feels like a sign of weakness?
- Do you sabotage your long-term goals because short-term discomfort feels overwhelming?

Let's be honest: grit doesn't mean you always feel strong. It means you show up anyway. If you're holding yourself back because you're waiting to feel confident, brave, or capable, you may be waiting forever. Grit is what carries you forward despite fear and doubt.

Grit also requires trust—in yourself, and in the process. You don't have to have everything figured out. You just have to be willing to take the next right step, even when the path is uncertain. The road to your dreams will not always be smooth, and that's okay. You're not aiming for perfection. You're choosing persistence.

## Building the Skill: Ways to Strengthen Your Grit

Grit is built through small, consistent choices—the more you lean into it, the more it becomes your natural response to difficulty. The following strategies can help you build endurance, emotional resilience, and the staying power to see your goals through.

1. **Acknowledge when you're struggling.**
   The first step to grit is not denial—it's honesty. Let yourself name the challenge and feel the emotions, but don't let them paralyze you.
2. **Set micro-goals.**
   Big goals are great, but they can feel overwhelming. Break them down into small, actionable steps, and then schedule them accordingly.
3. **Stick with your plan.**
   Grit lives in the follow-through. Progress comes from consistent effort, even if it takes three weeks or three years to achieve.

4. **Redefine failure.**

Every setback is feedback. Learn from it, and let it sharpen—not shatter—you.

5. **Ask for help.**

True grit doesn't mean going it alone. Whether you need emotional support, strategic advice, or mental health care, lean into your network.

6. **Choose perseverance over perfection.**

You don't need to be flawless. You need to be relentless.

7. **Visualize success.**

Spend a few minutes each day picturing yourself achieving your goal. Feel it. Believe it. This mental rehearsal fuels determination.

8. **Create accountability.**

Share your goal with someone you trust and let them check in on your progress. Sometimes, grit needs a witness.

Remember, grit isn't about being invincible—it's about being unwavering. When you put these strategies into practice, you'll start to recognize your own ability to rise and roar, again and again.

## Final Roar

You are not fragile. You are fierce.

You are not finished. You are forging forward.

You've got grit—and that's your superpower.

And when you look back one day, you'll see it clearly:

*Every time you kept going*
*when it would've been easier to stop—*
*that's what changed everything.*
*Not the loud wins. Not the applause.*
*But the quiet, gritty moments*
*when no one else was watching.*
*That's where your power lives.*
*In your perseverance.*
*In your rise.*

# Tenacious

## What It Means to Be Tenacious

The word tenacious comes from the Latin adjective *tenax*, meaning "persistent, clinging, or holding fast." In modern use, tenacious describes someone who doesn't readily relinquish a position or give up on a course of action. It's often used interchangeably with persistent and determined.

When you're tenacious, you're driven. You're willing to do the hard work. You care deeply about the result and are not afraid to show up fully committed to the outcome. Some may even call you an overachiever—and that's okay. What tenacity is not, however, is stubbornness. Stubbornness has a more rigid tone—it implies an unwillingness to accept change or consider alternate views. True tenacity is adaptable. A tenacious person can pivot, take feedback, and still stay the course toward the ultimate goal.

I'll never forget the first time someone called me tenacious—it was a former boss, and I was honestly offended. I thought he was calling me stubborn, and that did not sit well with me. I remember thinking, *Don't tell me I'm being difficult just because I'm pushing hard for something I believe in!*

But later that day, I calmed down enough to actually look up the word. And I realized he wasn't criticizing me—he was praising me. I had been passionately advocating for a particular direction that I felt, in my core, was right for our company. I wasn't willing to let it go, because I genuinely believed it would be a mistake to go any other way. I was fighting hard, but with intent. That wasn't stubbornness. That was tenacity.

Looking back, I realize that moment reshaped how I saw myself. I wasn't being difficult. I was being *driven*. I wasn't pushing for control—I was pushing for clarity, for alignment, for what I knew in my gut was the right path forward. That distinction matters.

> *Being tenacious doesn't mean*
> *refusing to budge just to be "right."*
> *It means refusing to give up when it matters.*

And I'm proud of that part of myself now.

As I reflect back on that incident with my manager, it struck me how easily we can misinterpret a compliment—especially when we're accustomed to being judged more harshly for our strengths. For a long time, I'd been conditioned to think that assertiveness was something to tone down. So when someone saw it and named it *tenacious*, I assumed it was a flaw. But sometimes, what we perceive as criticism is actually recognition. The problem isn't that we're "too much"—it's that we've been taught to see our power as a problem.

But when we start to recognize our perceived flaws as hidden compliments, we begin to unlock the full force of our tenacious lioness power.

## Are You Holding Yourself Back?

Let's get real: being tenacious isn't always celebrated—especially for women. We're often praised for being "easygoing," "flexible," and "collaborative," but when we hold firm to an idea or refuse to back down, suddenly we're labeled "difficult" or "too much." It's a double standard that many of us are all too familiar with.

But here's the thing—your ability to stay the course, to push through doubt, discomfort, and resistance, is a superpower. And yet, it's easy to confuse tenacity with other patterns that can hold us back, like perfectionism, burnout, or fear of letting go.

Take a moment and ask yourself:

- Do I give up too quickly when things get uncomfortable, assuming it must not be "meant to be"?
- Do I avoid difficult conversations or decisions because they might make others uncomfortable?
- Do I persist with something that's not working because I don't want to admit it's time to pivot?
- Am I mistaking rigidity for resilience?

Tenacity doesn't mean bulldozing your way through every obstacle without pause. It means staying committed with discernment. It's knowing when to dig in—and when to adapt. You can be strong and wise. You can be firm and flexible. You can be all in—and still be open to change. As one leader once told me during a high-stakes project: "It's an 'and' proposition, not an 'either/or.'" That phrase stuck with me—and shaped how I lead today.

We live in a world that often applauds compromise, even when it costs us clarity. But not every moment is meant to be softened. Tenacity sometimes looks like saying "no", setting a boundary, or simply staying silent when you're being pressured to back down. Holding your ground doesn't make you difficult—it makes you discerning.

Take a moment and ask yourself:

What's one moment I'm proud of where I stayed true to my values, even when it was uncomfortable?

If you've been holding back your voice, your ambition, or your truth because you're afraid of being "too much," hear this:

*You are not too much.*
*You are just enough—*
*and more than capable*
*of holding fast to what matters.*

# Building the Skill: How to Strengthen Your Tenacity

Let's talk about how to build tenacity in real life—because this isn't just theory. It's a skill you can practice.

You don't need to be born with an iron will to become tenacious. Steadfastness—the ability to remain firm and unwavering in the face of obstacles—is something you can develop and strengthen over time. Here are some powerful, practical ways to cultivate and sustain your steadfastness:

1. **Know what you're fighting for.**
   Tenacity without direction leads to burnout. Get clear on your why. When you know what truly matters to you, it's easier to stay committed and harder to get knocked off course.

2. **Listen without losing yourself.**
   A tenacious woman doesn't ignore feedback—she listens, learns, and then decides how to move forward. Let others' perspectives inform you, not derail you.

3. **Pause, don't quit.**
   When the weight feels too heavy, don't walk away just yet. Give yourself space to breathe, reset, and revisit. Tenacity sometimes means resting so you can rise again tomorrow.

4. **Set stretch goals.**
   Create short-term goals that challenge your endurance, not just your skill. Push your threshold little by little. Learn to stay in the hard place a bit longer each time.

5. **Celebrate every micro-victory.**
   Tenacity lives in the details—finishing the report, making the call, and confidently saying "no." Every small act of follow-through is a brick in your foundation.

6. **Define your non-negotiables.**
   What values or dreams are worth holding the line for, no matter what? Identify those unshakable priorities, principles, and values. Let them guide your decisions.

7. **Be willing to pivot.**

Tenacity isn't about going down with the ship—it's about steering the ship with clarity. Adapt when needed. Shift direction if it serves your purpose. The goal is growth, not martyrdom. And yes, sometimes tenacity means knowing when to pick your battles. You don't have to fight every hill to prove your strength—just the ones that matter.

Sometimes the strongest thing you can do is stay steady when everything else is shaking.

*Tenacity isn't about proving your worth.*
*It's about knowing it—*
*and holding steady when it counts.*
*You don't have to fight loudly to fight well.*

## Final Roar

Tenacity means being relentless, but with heart. It means being flexible and adapting when a compromise is required. It's not about always being right, but knowing when to hold the line because it matters.

When you combine deep conviction with adaptability, you become the kind of woman who gets things done, no matter the obstacles. Tenacity is your anchor in uncertainty and your engine when the road is long. It's how you rise, over and over again.

You are not here to be passive.

You are here to persevere.

To rise with purpose.

To stand in your truth.

To hold fast to what matters most.

*Let this be your truth:*

You are tenacious.

You adapt. You endure. You overcome.

And that makes you unstoppable.

# Brave

## What It Means to Be Brave

The word brave often conjures images of superheroes in capes or historic figures like Anne Frank—people who faced unimaginable challenges with unwavering courage. And while those are powerful and valid examples, they're not the only ones. Acts of bravery happen around us—and within us—every single day.

Bravery is deeply personal. It's not about grand gestures or public displays of courage. It's about the quiet, often unnoticed moments when we choose to step outside our comfort zone. The word brave has its roots in the Latin word *bravus*, meaning "bold" or "wild." This origin captures something important: bravery is not about the absence of fear, but about boldly stepping forward, even when fear is present. It's about making wild and determined choices in the face of uncertainty, discomfort, or risk.

Bravery doesn't always announce itself with fanfare. It's often quiet, personal, and deeply significant. It's the parent navigating the challenges of raising a child, the student speaking up in class, or the professional taking a stand in a meeting. As adults, we sometimes overlook the many acts of bravery we perform each day simply by showing up, speaking out, or trying something new. However, it's essential to acknowledge and celebrate these moments, as they serve as a testament to our courage and resilience.

Being brave is about reaching outside your comfort zone, whether slightly or drastically. It's saying "yes" to an opportunity that scares you. It's having the courage to stand up for something you believe in or to push back when someone crosses a line. Bravery is not about being fearless—it's about being willing to act even when fear tries to hold you back.

In the workplace, bravery often shows up as advocacy and voice. As a woman in leadership, I can't count the number of times I've been spoken over or dismissed by male colleagues in meetings. It often happens without the other person even realizing it, but the impact is real. I remember a recent workshop where this happened to me. I was sharing a point when a male peer interrupted and completely redirected the conversation. My words hung in the air, unfinished. And do you know what I did?

Nothing.

I didn't speak up or call it out. Not because I didn't notice—but *because I was tired.* Tired of always having to fight harder just to be heard. Tired of being labeled as too "assertive" or "pushy" for simply wanting respect. The brave thing to do in that moment would have been to say, "Excuse me, I wasn't finished. You just spoke over me." But I didn't. And that's okay. I've learned to give myself grace for moments when I didn't rise to the occasion.

Still, I want you to do what I wish I had done: Speak up, push back, and don't accept being dismissed or disrespected. In those moments, bravery isn't about confrontation—it's about integrity. It's about valuing your voice and your presence enough to stand in them, even when they shake. And while some people may not realize they're interrupting or dismissing others, calling it out—respectfully—is still necessary. Sometimes, bravery means helping others see what they couldn't on their own.

Be brave. Be bold. And speak up for what is right—even when it's uncomfortable.

## Are You Holding Yourself Back?

Bravery is not the absence of fear—*it's moving forward in spite of it.*

But often, we don't even realize the ways we're holding ourselves back from being brave. We rationalize our silence or convince ourselves that the risk is too high. We minimize our voice, shrink our presence, or stay small to avoid discomfort or conflict. We forget that being brave doesn't mean being loud—it just means being present.

**You may be braver than you think.**

Bravery doesn't always look like a battle cry. Sometimes it looks like a breath, a boundary, or a steady, quiet *no*. The truth is, you've probably already shown bravery in ways you haven't even named.

Here are a few ways you may already be choosing bravery over comfort:

- You speak up, even when your voice shakes.
- You risk being misunderstood and speak with honesty.
- You ask the hard question in a room that prefers silence.
- You let someone down in order to stay true to yourself.

And if you're wondering where you may still be holding back, ask yourself:

- Do I silence myself in meetings or conversations because I fear judgment or backlash?
- Am I avoiding taking a stand on something important because I fear confrontation?
- Have I convinced myself that someone else will speak up, so I don't have to?
- Do I wait for perfect conditions before I try something new?
- Do I believe that being brave only applies to "big" moments, and therefore dismiss my own courage?
- Have I ever told myself: *It's not worth the fight,* when deep down I knew I should have said something?

Sometimes, the bravest thing we can do is admit we're tired of always fighting. And that's okay. But bravery doesn't require us to be fearless, loud, or relentless. It requires us to choose action when it counts. The moment you recognize a pattern of holding back, that's the exact moment to lean into your courage.

# Building the Skill: Strategies to Be Brave

Bravery is a glowing ember inside each one of us—quiet, steady, and full of potential. With care, intention, and small daily acts, that ember becomes a flame. Here are ways to tend to your own bravery:

1. **Start with micro-bravery.**
   Bravery doesn't have to be epic. Speak up in a meeting, ask a question you're nervous about, or try something unfamiliar. Each small act builds your confidence.

2. **Name your fear.**
   Write it down or say it out loud. "I'm afraid they'll think I'm too aggressive." "I'm scared of being wrong." Once you name it, you take away some of its power.

3. **Reframe the outcome.**
   Don't fixate on *What if I fail?* Instead, ask, *What if I succeed?* or *What will I regret more—trying and failing, or not trying at all?*

4. **Use role-play or scripting.**
   If you struggle with speaking up, practice what you'd say. "I'd like to finish my thought before we move on." The more you rehearse, the more natural it becomes.

5. **Find brave role models.**
   Identify people in your life or in history who embody everyday bravery. Let their stories remind you that courage comes in many forms.

6. **Celebrate your brave moments.**
   Write them down. Reflect on them. Give yourself credit for even the smallest acts of courage. They matter, and they deserve to be acknowledged and celebrated.

7. **Speak up even when your voice shakes.**

That's the very definition of bravery. Use your voice, even when it feels hard. Especially when it feels hard.

Bravery isn't about the absence of fear—it's about the willingness to act anyway.

The more you show up for yourself in the small moments, the easier it becomes to rise in the big ones. Every time you speak with honesty, stand in your truth, or move forward despite your nerves, you're strengthening that inner flame.

These practices aren't just about bravery in the workplace or on a stage.

They're about the courage it takes to be real in your relationships, to set boundaries, to ask for help, and to chase dreams that scare you just a little. Bravery is a muscle—and you're already building it, one bold moment at a time.

## Final Roar

*Bravery begins with a whisper*
*and builds with every bold step you take.*

Bravery doesn't always shout.

Sometimes it whispers, *Try again tomorrow.*

It's not about perfection—it's about presence and persistence.

It's the decision to stand in your truth, use your voice, and push past fear even when you're tired.

It's in the quiet moments when you choose yourself, choose justice, choose to speak.

I've learned that being brave doesn't mean I always get it right. It means I don't give up. I reflect. I rise. I roar again.

***So the next time fear tries to quiet you, remember this:***
You don't have to be fearless to be brave.
You just have to be willing.
And if your voice shakes? Let it.
That's still brave. That still counts.

# (S)hero

## What It Means to Be a (S)hero

Most *(S)heroes* don't wear capes.

They don't stand on podiums or make headlines. They aren't always the loudest in the room. More often, they're the women quietly doing the work—holding things together, speaking the truth when it's hard, lifting others up, and showing up when it matters most.

The word *(S)hero* is a blend of *she* and *hero*—a reminder that women have always been part of the hero narrative, even when history left us out of the headlines. You'll see me use the word throughout this chapter, but I've kept the chapter title as *(S)hero* to make that inclusion visible. From here on, I'll use Shero to honor the everyday women who lead with courage, purpose, and heart.

A Shero isn't defined by fame. She's defined by impact.

She's the one who stays late to mentor a colleague who doubts herself.

The one who insists that a friend get that mammogram.

The one who speaks up in a meeting—not for credit, but because the truth needs a voice.

She's the mom working two jobs who still shows up for her daughter's school play with tired eyes and a cheering heart.

She's the woman who walks away from a toxic relationship and rebuilds from the ground up.

She's the caregiver tending to her aging parents while balancing her own dreams, often on the edge of exhaustion.

She's the one who comforts a friend, organizes a food drive, or dares to say, "This isn't okay"—even when it would be easier to stay quiet.

Sometimes, she's also the one who's been knocked down, faced the diagnosis, lost the job, or buried a dream—and found the strength to rise anyway.

I've come to believe that Sheroism isn't something we strive for. It's something we grow into—through experience, through courage, and through choice. We become Sheroes not by chasing the spotlight, but by owning our influence and using it with clarity and conviction.

That legacy runs deep.

The word Shero dates back to at least the 1800s, during the early days of the women's suffrage movement. Even then, women were leading revolutions, fighting for change, and redefining what leadership looked like—long before society gave them the credit they deserved.

I think of Rosa Parks, quietly taking a stand by staying seated. It was not a popular action, but her courage sparked a movement that changed the course of history. I think of Ruth Bader Ginsburg, the "Notorious RBG," whose sharp mind and relentless advocacy opened doors for women and for marginalized communities everywhere. These women didn't act for fame—they simply refused to stay silent. They stood up, spoke out, and paved the way for the rest of us.

Their Sheroism wasn't about ego. It was about integrity.

And while their names live in history, there are countless unnamed Sheroes walking among us every day—including you and me.

In my own life, I've seen glimpses of this same quiet courage.

First, I use my voice to create space for others. In work meetings and social settings, I pay attention to who's being overlooked and make it a point to say: "Let's hear her out."

Second, I advocate fiercely for women's health. As a breast cancer survivor, I know the power of self-advocacy. I've learned that one conversation can be life-saving, and sometimes the most Sheroic thing we can do is simply remind someone we care about to take action.

None of this makes me exceptional. It just makes me *aware*—aware of the responsibility we all carry, and the difference we can make when we choose to lead with purpose.

That's what makes a Shero: not a title you earn once, but a lifelong journey of rising, reaching, and showing up—with courage, compassion, and the commitment to become an even bolder version of yourself.

## Are You Holding Yourself Back?

Many women don't see themselves as Sheroes because they think they must be famous, lead a movement, or wear a cape.

*But a Shero isn't defined by headlines—she's defined by her actions.*

If you've ever helped someone speak up, protected your health fiercely, mentored another woman, or stood your ground when it mattered—you are a Shero.

Still, too many women hesitate to claim that power. We've been conditioned to see influence as something reserved for others—those with louder voices, bigger platforms, or more credentials. But real influence? It starts in the choices you make every day.

Here are a few questions to reflect on:

- Are you downplaying your influence because you think it's "not big enough"?
- Do you hesitate to speak up, even when you know someone needs your voice?
- Are you dismissing your own struggles and victories, assuming they don't matter?

*Sheroes are ordinary women*
*who make extraordinary choices.*
*And that includes you.*

But here's the truth: we need more women to recognize the power they already have.

To speak up when it's uncomfortable.

To take the lead even when they feel unprepared.

To call out injustice.

To reach back and pull another woman forward.

This is how we shift culture—not through one grand gesture, but through a thousand small acts of courage.

It's not enough to believe in your own potential—you have to hype up the women around you, too. Celebrate their wins. Speak their names in rooms they're not in. Be the woman who says, "You've got this," when someone doubts themselves.

Every time you choose to support rather than compete, uplift rather than judge, or encourage rather than criticize—you're acting as a Shero.

And the world needs more of that.

The world needs more of *you*.

## Building the Skill: How to Step into Your Inner Shero

You don't wake up one day and suddenly feel like a Shero. You become one—through choices, habits, and acts of courage, both big and small. Whether it's mentoring a colleague, using your voice in a tough moment, or simply refusing to stay silent, each of these moments adds to your story. The following strategies aim to help you recognize the power you already possess and harness that power with intention.

1. **Learn from legacy.**

   Take time to read about women in history who broke barriers. Their courage is a blueprint—and a reminder that change often starts with one person taking one brave step.

2. **Lift others as you rise.**

   A Shero doesn't rise alone. She opens doors for others. At work, in your community, or at home—ask yourself: "Who can I empower today?"

3. **Advocate fiercely.**
   Whether it's for your health, your rights, or someone else's, don't be afraid to challenge the status quo. If something feels off, it probably is—say something.

4. **Own your story.**
   The battles you've fought and the wisdom you've gained are worth sharing. Speak openly about what you've overcome—your story could be the survival guide for someone else.

5. **Be someone's spark.**
   Sometimes, all it takes is a kind word, a shared resource, or an "I believe in you" to ignite change in someone else's life. That spark? That's Shero work.

You don't have to wait for a perfect moment or a grand stage to be a Shero.

Every day offers an opportunity to lead with courage, to take a stand, or to lift someone else.

It's in these everyday moments that your power is revealed—and your legacy begins.

> *The world doesn't need flawless leaders.*
> *It needs women who care deeply, act bravely,*
> *and choose to rise again and again.*
> *That's what makes you a Shero.*

## Final Roar

Being a Shero isn't about perfection. It's about presence. It's about showing up with integrity, using your influence for good, and being willing to take action—even when no one's watching. You are stronger than you think. And the more you step into your power, the more permission you give others to do the same.

You don't need a cape to be a Shero. You just need courage, compassion, and a commitment to doing what's right—even when it's hard. Whether you're marching in protest, mentoring a colleague, or reminding a friend to schedule her mammogram—you're already leading with intention and heart.

*Your actions matter.*
*Your voice matters.*
*You matter.*

# Resilient

## What It Means to Be Resilient

I never considered myself resilient—at least, not until I started reflecting on what the word truly means. The word resilient comes from the Latin *resilire*, meaning "to spring back" or "rebound." That image—a spring snapping back into shape—feels both accurate and incomplete. Because real-life resilience isn't instantaneous, it's not a perfect return to form. It's messy. It's painful. It's slow. And it doesn't mean the pain disappears. What it does mean is that you summon the courage to keep moving forward, even when your world has shattered. You bend, but you do not break. You get back up—again and again—until one day, you find yourself standing in the light again.

When I think through my life experiences, the one that tested me most deeply—heart, mind, and soul—was the death of my father.

When I was growing up, my dad's side of the family would gather every Thanksgiving—grandparents, aunts, uncles, cousins. We weren't a huge family, maybe 20–25 people, but the love and laughter filled every room. In 1989, we had what felt like a perfect holiday. The cousins were all close in age—we played games, shared stories, and sat elbow-to-elbow around long tables. None of us realized it would be our last Thanksgiving with my father.

Unbeknownst to me at the time, my parents had recently discovered a lump under my dad's arm. I don't remember if it had been biopsied by Thanksgiving, but I now know they were already worried. Still, they didn't say anything that day. They let us laugh. They let us be joyful. I was in my final year of college, and my brother had just welcomed his first child. Everything felt normal. Everything felt okay.

Then came the news, sometime shortly after the holidays. Stage 4 renal cell carcinoma. No viable treatment options. My dad bravely decided to join a clinical trial, knowing it likely wouldn't save him, but hoping it would help someone else someday. That was who he was—always thinking of others.

I didn't want to believe it. I couldn't. So I buried myself in school. I overloaded my schedule, trying to keep moving, trying to stay ahead of the grief I knew was waiting to catch up to me. When spring break came, I drove home, desperate to see my dad but emotionally spent. I stayed for a few days, but then, at his urging, I left to visit a friend in Chicago. Looking back, I believe he knew his time was near—he didn't want me to witness his final moments. He tried to protect me, even at the end.

My dad passed away while I was on that trip. I didn't get to say goodbye in the way I wanted. But I know, without a doubt, that he gave me a gift. He gave me permission to keep living.

The rest of that year felt like a fog. I overloaded my schedule—23 credit hours, two degrees, independent study hours—because drowning in studies and schoolwork felt easier than drowning in grief.

But the truth is, I was barely functioning. I shut down. I isolated myself. I couldn't breathe in a world where my dad didn't exist.

I wrote to cope. I poured my heart into a song called *"You Are The One"*—a piece I still haven't released, but one that carried me through some of my darkest hours. It was my cry to God—my way of reaching for something greater than myself during a time when I felt utterly alone. And honestly, the only way I knew how to scream at the unfairness of life was through music. The chorus gave me life when I had none:

> *"You are the One who can carry me through,*
> *when the storms of life overwhelm me."*
> —Ronda K. Salazar, *original song lyric*

I found refuge in *Footprints in the Sand*—an anonymous poem about God carrying us during our lowest times. God wasn't just walking beside me—He was cradling me when I couldn't stand on my own.

And slowly—day by day, choice by choice—I came back to life.

It wasn't overnight, and it wasn't graceful. It was messy. It was real.

It took almost three years of stumbling, rising, learning, and breaking through.

*But I kept going. Because I am resilient.*

And I knew my dad, who always called me "Little Miss Muffet," would want me to keep going. And I did.

## Are You Holding Yourself Back?

Resilience doesn't always come with a battle cry or a breakthrough moment. Sometimes it's quiet. Sometimes it's messy. Often, it's unnoticed by others.

We often think we need to bounce back quickly or stay strong for everyone else. But real resilience isn't about holding it all together—it's about allowing yourself to fall apart and still choosing to get back up. It's not a flawless return to form; it's an honest, courageous decision to keep going, even when the pieces don't fit like they used to.

And that decision? It doesn't have to be dramatic. Sometimes it's as simple as getting out of bed when your heart is broken. Sometimes it's saying no when you're exhausted or choosing to rest instead of pushing through. That's resilience, too.

If you're not giving yourself credit for the ways you've already survived, maybe it's time to pause and notice just how far you've come.

Ask yourself:

- Are you giving yourself permission to grieve and grow?
- Are you waiting for a magical moment of motivation instead of taking just one next step?
- Are you measuring your healing by someone else's timeline?
- Do you carry shame for how long it's taken you to "get over" something?

Resilience isn't about perfection or speed. It's about showing up again, especially with the scars. It's about staying soft in a world that tried to harden you. If you're holding yourself back because you think resilience has to look strong and composed, let that go.

Sometimes the strongest thing you can do is simply whisper: *I'm still here.*

## Building the Skill: Strategies to Strengthen Your Resilience

Resilience isn't just something you either have or don't—it's something you build. Through the most challenging times in life, there are tools and choices that can help you recover, rise, and reclaim your strength. Here are a few strategies that helped me, and might help you too.

1. **Allow the breakdown.**
   Let yourself feel. Cry. Collapse. Rant. Release. The breakdown often creates the conditions for the breakthrough.
2. **Create meaning through expression.**
   Write, paint, sing, or speak your pain. Your creativity can be a lifeline. (That song I wrote? That was resilience in action.)
3. **Anchor yourself in purpose or faith.**
   When everything feels out of control, lean into something bigger than yourself—whether it's God, purpose, nature, or community.
4. **Practice micro-recovery.**
   You don't have to bounce all the way back in one leap. Focus on small wins: a shower, a walk, a phone call.
5. **Reach out—even when it's hard.**
   Isolating can feel safe, but healing thrives in connection. Find one person you trust and let them in. You're not alone in this journey, and reaching out is a sign of strength, not weakness.

6. **Set gentle milestones.**

   Progress doesn't mean forgetting—it means remembering with more peace than pain. Celebrate each step toward wholeness.

7. **Visualize your future self.**

   Picture the version of you who made it through this. What would she tell you right now? Let her wisdom guide your next step.

Resilience isn't linear—and it doesn't look the same for everyone. The tools that help you today might not have helped you yesterday. And that's okay. The beauty of resilience is that it evolves with you. What matters most is not how quickly you bounce back, but how intentionally you choose to keep moving forward.

There is no right way to heal. There is only *your* way—step by step, choice by choice. The more you honor your journey, the more fully you'll reclaim your strength. Let each strategy be a reminder: you are not powerless in your pain. You are rebuilding something stronger. And that, in itself, is a powerful act of resilience.

## Final Roar

Resilience isn't a perfect path. It's messy, uncertain and full of detours. It doesn't always come with clarity or certainty. Often, it's forged in the darkest moments—when the pain feels unbearable and the weight of loss or struggle threatens to crush your spirit.

*It's in those moments,*
*when you choose to put one foot in front of the other,*
*that true resilience is born.*

The process is painful.  It can leave you raw, cracked open, and unsure. But when you push through that pain—when you refuse to let it define you—you slowly begin to rise.

And on the other side of that pain is light.

It may not look like the light you once knew, but it's there.

It's healing. It's hope.

**And it's yours to walk into.**

So if today you are crawling, not standing—keep going.

If today you feel broken, not brave—keep going.

Because resilience lives in the very act of not giving up.

You are not just surviving.

You are becoming.

And that is the most powerful kind of strength there is.

# Unstoppable

## What It Means to Be Unstoppable

The word unstoppable is such an incredibly powerful word. Just saying it out loud commands and demands respect. It doesn't whisper. It doesn't ask politely. It roars. When I say *unstoppable*, I feel it in my chest. It's a word I've claimed as my own—a personal anthem and affirmation of my power and control.

*I am an unstoppable force of creativity.*

*I am an unstoppable force of leadership.*

You can try it, too:

*I am an unstoppable force of* _____. Fill in the blank with whatever lights your fire.

For me, unstoppable implies that nothing—*nothing*—can prevent me from completing what I set my mind to. I don't just dabble or wait for permission. I don't take detours. I move forward with grit and conviction. I act #WithPurpose.

And here's the thing: I've realized I've been subconsciously applying the word unstoppable to almost everything I do in life. There is no ceiling I accept, no barrier I won't find a way through. If something's in my way, it better move, because I am moving through it. Sometimes, just whispering the word to myself during a chaotic day is enough to lift me above the noise, the pettiness, the distraction: *I am unstoppable. Get out of my way.*

To me, unstoppable and determined are sister words. They go hand in hand. One fuels the other. And when I think about what truly tested that unstoppable spirit, one moment in particular rises to the surface.

When I was diagnosed with breast cancer, my world stopped—or so I thought. That word—*cancer*—hits like a freight train. In that moment, I honestly thought my life was over. That's where my head went: fear, finality, the unknown.

But then came my brother Ron.

We were working in the same building in downtown St. Louis at the time. After I got the diagnosis, a friend grabbed my brother, and he did what big brothers do best—he showed up. He took me across the street to a Starbucks. I was falling apart, completely undone. And he sat there with me, not trying to fix it, not trying to sugarcoat it—just being there. He cracked jokes, let me cry, gave me space to grieve, and then, as only a big brother could do, he got down to business.

We started talking about an action plan—because that's what people in my family do. That's how we are wired.

And then he said something I'll never forget (paraphrased): "We gotta do what Gines's always do—we dive in, define our plan, and move forward. We act—we don't sit back." (*Gines is my maiden name.*)

That was it. That was the reminder I needed. That was the moment I remembered who I was: a woman who doesn't retreat, a woman who tackles everything head-on, a woman who does everything #*WithPurpose*.

But even the most unstoppable woman sometimes needs a moment to pause—and receive. During that chapter of my life, Howard, my partner at the time, became my rock. We had been together for years, bonded by our love of music and a deep mutual respect. And when cancer brought my independence to a halt, Howard stepped in with unwavering strength and tenderness. He helped me when I couldn't help myself. After my bilateral mastectomy, I couldn't even lift my arms. I had to rebuild my body from the inside out—literally. Howard was there for the hard days, the vulnerable moments, the slow healing. He encouraged me, reminded me of who I was, and most of all, loved me—new scars and all.

He taught me something I hadn't fully learned yet: that letting your guard down is not weakness—it's wisdom. That even a strong, confident, independent woman can lean on someone else without losing herself. Howard helped me heal. We're no longer together, but he's still my best friend—and still my biggest cheerleader. I will always be grateful for the way he helped this unstoppable woman take a brief, necessary pause—so she could rise again even stronger.

That mindset carried me through cancer and out the other side. Like everything else in my life, I took on the "C" word, and I didn't stop pushing forward—not until I had conquered it. I was unstoppable then, and I am unstoppable now.

## Are You Holding Yourself Back?

Let's get honest. There are so many ways we can block our own forward momentum and prevent ourselves from having an unstoppable mindset. Here are a few examples to consider:

- Do you stop yourself before you even start?
- Do you talk yourself out of big ideas before they have a chance to breathe?
- Do you hear a voice that says, "Who do you think you are?" every time you try to rise up?

That voice is not your truth—it's your fear. And fear has a very specific job: to keep you small.

*But you were never meant to play small.*
*You were never meant to stay silent.*

Being unstoppable doesn't mean you don't get scared. It means you move anyway, facing the fear, staring it down, and taking action with purpose. When I need a boost of fierce energy, I channel my inner Xena Warrior Princess or Wonder Woman—two icons of unapologetic, powerful, (S)hero-level fierceness. They remind me that strength doesn't always look soft or quiet. Sometimes, it's wild, untamed, and exactly what the moment demands.

It's okay to be scared, but it's not okay to let fear hold you back.

Ask yourself:

- What am I letting stop me right now?
- Whose permission am I waiting for?
- What would I do if I believed I was truly unstoppable?

You don't need all the answers. You just need the next step—and the willingness to take it.

## Building the Skill: How to Reinforce an Unstoppable Mindset

You can take several actions to help strengthen your mindset and become an unstoppable force, thereby unleashing your inner lioness. Here's how:

1. **Anchor your affirmation.**

   Declare it boldly: *I am an unstoppable force of* _____. Fill in the blank with your focus: love, innovation, healing, impact. Use it as a mantra—daily, hourly if needed. Let it become part of your rhythm.

2. **Make your moves bold and intentional.**

   Don't wait. Don't shrink. If an opportunity arises and aligns with your purpose, seize it. If there's a challenge that scares you, take it on intentionally. Your progress doesn't have to be perfect—it just has to be in motion.

3. **Use your story as fuel.**

   When doubt creeps in, remind yourself what you've already overcome. Let your history of resilience become the launchpad for your next brave step. You've faced storms before, and you're still standing.

4. **Surround yourself with unstoppable energy.**
   Be mindful of who's in your circle. Surround yourself with people who push forward, who lift you up, who remind you of your power—not those who make you question it.
5. **Act like the unstoppable force you already are.**
   This is not a wish or a future version of you—it's already in your DNA. You just have to own it.

*Every bold move,*
*every fierce choice,*
*every moment you refuse to quit—*
*that's how you build your unstoppable mindset.*

## Final Roar

You were not born to pause, play small, or retreat.
You were born to rise, to lead, to impact, to blaze trails.
And to do it all *#WithPurpose.*
You are unstoppable.
**Step into it. Rise with it. Lead with it.**

# IV

# Lead with Vision

# Purpose and Impact

Leadership doesn't start with a title. It begins with a sense of purpose and a vision for what's possible. This part of the book is about stepping into your power, not just for yourself, but to create a positive impact for others. In Part IV, words like *Purposeful, Visionary, Waymaker,* and *Transforming* will empower you to lead with authenticity, speak with purpose, and align your actions with your deeper mission.

Too often, women wait for permission to lead. We question whether we're ready, experienced enough, or qualified. But leadership is not about perfection. It's about showing up fully, with clarity, courage, and compassion. It's about being brave enough to light the way—even when you're still figuring it out yourself.

You don't have to have it all together to be a leader. And it's not just about leadership in a work or professional setting. It's about leading in every aspect of your life. It's about caring enough to speak up, contribute, and lift others. Caring enough to stand for something bigger than yourself. And caring enough to keep going, even when it's hard.

This section invites you to reimagine leadership—not as something reserved for the few, but as a daily choice to live *#WithPurpose* and act with intention. Whether you're leading a team, a family, a movement, or simply your own life, these words will help you lead from within.

This is your invitation to lead from the inside out—to rediscover who you are when you stop performing and start aligning. As you turn these pages, you'll be challenged to reflect, to stretch, and to reclaim the parts of yourself that may have been silenced or overlooked. This is where leadership becomes personal. Where purpose and identity meet. Where your transformation doesn't just serve others—it brings *you* home to yourself.

Let these words guide you toward a deeper purpose. Let them fuel your impact.

Leadership begins in the quiet moments—when you dare to imagine something better and take one small step toward it.

Lead boldly. The world needs your vision.

# Deliberate

## What It Means to Be Deliberate

The word deliberate has always fascinated me. At first glance, it can seem rigid or even negative, like something done with cold calculation or hidden malice. But over time, I've come to see this word as a quiet superpower. Not loud. Not flashy. But unshakable.

Deliberate comes from the Latin *deliberatus*, meaning "weighed carefully." I love that image—holding a decision in your hands like a set of old-fashioned scales, measuring every option carefully. It isn't about hesitation. It's about honor. It's about treating your choices—and your impact on others—with respect.

In my leadership role, I'm often expected to make decisions quickly. There isn't always time for long analysis or consensus-building. But that doesn't mean I abandon intention. In fact, even in fast-paced environments, I've learned how to be deliberate. How? I know my values. I trust my instincts. And I've trained myself to pause—just long enough to align my actions with what matters.

But this hasn't always been easy.

Very early in my career, in my twenties, I was in a new position and tasked with overseeing a major software rollout for a new client. I was still learning the ins and outs of our system, but I was eager to prove myself. So, when I led a meeting with the client to outline deliverables, I overpromised—badly. I informed them that a critical new feature—a feature still a year away from being ready—would be included in their rollout.

I thought saying yes quickly and delivering fast would make me look capable and confident. But in my rush to impress, I skipped the hard part—asking questions, checking facts, and weighing the long-term impact of that promise.

It wasn't until we were in the final stages of client training that someone asked about the feature—and my stomach dropped.

In all the hustle, I had genuinely forgotten the promise I'd made.

We double-checked, hoping I was wrong, but the feature wasn't ready—and wouldn't be for months.

The client had built their plans around it.

The launch had to be delayed while our developers scrambled to catch up.

I was mortified.

But more than that—I was changed.

That single moment shifted how I approached every decision from that point forward. I learned that urgency is not the same as clarity. That speed isn't a substitute for integrity. And that being deliberate doesn't mean being slow—it means being sure.

Over time, I began to lead differently. To pause. To weigh the ripple effects. To ask better questions.

Today, I live my life by the phrase #WithPurpose. It's more than a mantra—it's a commitment. To act with intention. To speak with care. To lead with integrity. Whether I'm deciding how to spend an hour or how to respond to a crisis, I strive to be deliberate.

Because when you move deliberately, you don't just make decisions.

You make a difference.

## Are You Holding Yourself Back?

Sometimes, we avoid being deliberate because we lack confidence in ourselves. We fear failure or are unsure what the "right" next step is. But inaction is still a decision. And it rarely leads to empowerment.

Ask yourself this:

- Do you second-guess your decisions—big or small?
- Do you find yourself paralyzed by indecision, fearing you'll make the "wrong" choice?
- Do you let others make the decisions for you, telling yourself it's easier that way?
- Do you delay action until you feel 100% ready—even if that moment never comes?
- Do you look to others for permission before trusting your own instincts?
- Do you fear that choosing one path means abandoning all others—and therefore chose none?

Being deliberate doesn't require perfection. It requires presence. You have to be willing to engage with the moment, evaluate your priorities, and then take a stand. Let go of the myth that there is always one right answer.

And here's the truth: You're going to make mistakes. We all do. But being deliberate doesn't mean avoiding failure—it means choosing to learn from it. Growth comes from reflection, not perfection. If fear of making the wrong move is keeping you frozen, remember: indecision is still a decision. And staying stuck is rarely the path to progress.

Your hesitation might be rooted in doubt or fear of judgment. But here's the reframe: What if being deliberate is not about control but about clarity? Not about being rigid, but about being rooted in your values?

If you've been holding back, waiting for a sign or the perfect moment, consider this: Maybe the power move is simply choosing. And doing it deliberately.

*I don't wait for the perfect moment.*
*I choose the one I'm in.*
*And I move forward—with purpose.*

## Building the Skill: How to Cultivate Being Deliberate

Deliberate decision-making isn't just about logic—it's about leadership.

It's the conscious choice to pause before you act, to align with your values before you speak, and to honor the weight of your decisions, no matter how small they seem. Building this skill takes practice, but it's one of the most empowering tools you can cultivate. The more deliberate you are, the more confident, capable, and grounded you become. These strategies will help you strengthen that mindset.

1. **Mindful pausing.**
   Before jumping into a response or choice, take one deep breath. A brief pause creates space for intentional thinking.
2. **Define your "why."**
   Before acting, ask: *What outcome am I hoping for? What value is this decision rooted in?* When you know your "why," your "what" becomes clearer.
3. **Create a simple decision matrix.**
   When facing a difficult choice, jot down the pros and cons. Include both emotional and logical considerations. This helps you see the decision from all angles without becoming stuck.
4. **Make peace with imperfection.**
   No decision is foolproof. Instead of agonizing over the perfect path, choose the one that feels most aligned and commit to it—with intention.
5. **Reflect after an action.**
   After a decision, take a few moments to reflect. What worked? What didn't? How did being deliberate help? This reflective process builds your confidence and insight for next time.

***The world may try to rush you,***
***but your power lies in the pause.***

When you choose to be deliberate, you choose presence over pressure. You become an individual who leads not by accident, but with courage and intention. So breathe. Think. Decide. And walk boldly in the direction that honors your truth.

## Final Roar

Being deliberate is not about overthinking—it's about respecting the power of your choices.

Sometimes, the most powerful move is the one you *don't* rush. The pause, the breath, the moment of clarity—that's where your wisdom lives. Being deliberate means slowing down just enough to align with what truly matters.

You don't have to prove yourself through urgency. You prove yourself by choosing to move with clarity, presence, and purpose—even when no one's watching.

When you lead with intention, you lead with impact. Whether the moment is big or small, trust yourself to choose boldly, clearly, and with intention. Let this mantra guide your next step.

***Mantra for the Deliberate Soul:***
I do not drift. I decide.
I move forward not by chance, but by choice.
Every step I take is made with intent.
I am a deliberate force of wisdom, clarity, and strength.

# Compelling

## What It Means to Be Compelling

Martin Luther King Jr. didn't just deliver a speech—he offered a vision. *"I Have A Dream"* was more than words; it was a call to conscience that echoed across generations. Malala Yousafzai, with a voice calm and unwavering, stood before global leaders and demanded education for every girl. Maya Angelou didn't shout—but when she spoke, the room stilled. What made these voices so powerful wasn't volume or perfection. It was conviction. It was clarity. It was presence.

That's what it means to be compelling.

The word compelling comes from the Latin *compellere*, meaning "to drive together" or "to urge with force." And in the context of communication, compelling people do precisely that—they draw others in, not by coercion, but by connection. They speak in ways that resonate. They lead in ways that inspire. They carry themselves with quiet force—not by dominating, but by embodying a message so rooted in truth that it becomes impossible to ignore.

Being compelling doesn't require a microphone or a stage. It requires alignment. When your message matches your presence—when your energy supports your words—you become magnetic. People lean in. They want to understand. They remember what you said and, most importantly, the emotion you left behind.

I still remember my first-grade teacher, Miss Canfield. I thought she was the most beautiful woman in the world—not because of how she looked, but because of the sense of safety and encouragement she gave me. I was just six years old, in my first real school, and she made me feel seen, supported, and capable. At the end of the year, we had a class contest, and one of the prizes was a 5x7 photo of Miss Canfield and a scrapbook. Of course, my competitive nature made sure that I won that prize. Somewhere, I still have that picture. She had a scarf tied around her neck, a perfect Dorothy Hamill haircut, and a smile full of kindness that could cut through anyone's bad day.

Miss Canfield was compelling, especially to an impressionable 6-year-old. She didn't give speeches or lead organizations. She shaped lives. Mine included. She showed me—before I had words for it—that women can make a difference in any job, any role, any moment, simply by being fully themselves.

Sometimes, the most compelling people never intend to lead—they simply live with such unwavering integrity that others can't help but follow. Their words align with their values. Their actions ripple outward. And their presence lingers, long after the moment has passed.

That's the kind of woman I aspire to be. Not polished to perfection, but anchored in purpose. Not needing the spotlight, but willing to speak up when it matters. That's what makes a voice compelling—not its volume, but its truth.

That's the heart of being compelling. It's not about being louder. It's about being rooted. It's about presence over performance, truth over polish, and passion over perfection. And the best part? It's a skill you can build—one grounded in alignment, authenticity, and bold clarity.

Who was the Miss Canfield in your life—the person whose presence moved you, even if they didn't try to? Let yourself remember her. Let that memory remind you of the quiet power **you** already carry as a direct result of her compelling authenticity.

# Are You Holding Yourself Back?

Let's be honest—being compelling isn't something most of us were taught. In fact, many of us were raised to "be nice," "don't speak too boldly," or "don't ruffle feathers." We were encouraged to be agreeable, even if it meant staying quiet when we had something valuable to say. That conditioning runs deep—and it often shows up in meetings, interviews, presentations, and even everyday conversations.

Ask yourself:

- Have you ever caught yourself downplaying your ideas?
- Do you find yourself softening your voice or apologizing before you speak?
- Do you avoid eye contact while making a valid point—just to avoid seeming "too confident" or "too much"?

These habits may feel small, but they dilute your message and your presence. You might be holding yourself back by assuming your voice doesn't matter— or worse, that it's not welcome.

Here's the truth: you don't need permission to be powerful. You don't need validation to speak with authority. And you definitely don't need to shrink yourself to be accepted.

Being compelling means showing up fully. It means owning your voice, your story, and your presence. You already have something to say. The question is—will you say it like you believe it?

If you're still struggling to step into that power, ask yourself:

- Are you speaking in a way that invites others to take you seriously?
- Are you allowing your passion to come through—or are you muting yourself?
- Are you over-explaining or justifying, instead of simply stating?

Don't let fear of judgment, discomfort, or rejection rob you of your influence. You don't have to be loud. You don't have to be perfect. You just have to speak from a place of truth and intention.

That's what makes someone compelling.

## Building the Skill: How to Be More Compelling

If being compelling feels like a stretch for you, the good news is this: it's a skill you can build. With practice and intention, your presence, voice, and message can become more powerful and magnetic. Here's how to start:

1. **Lead with presence.**
   Before you say a word, your presence speaks for you. Walk into the room (or open the Zoom call) with grounded energy. Take a breath. Make eye contact. Be intentional about how you enter and engage—people will notice.

2. **Speak with clarity and purpose.**
   Before speaking, ask yourself: *What's the key point I want to communicate?* Then say it simply and clearly. Skip the fluff. People remember clarity—not complexity.

3. **Practice persuasive storytelling.**
   Facts inform, but stories move people. Learn to share vivid, real-life examples that blend logic and emotion. The best communicators know how to speak to both the heart and the mind.

4. **Make eye contact and engage.**
   Whether in a room or on a video call, maintaining eye contact builds trust. It signals confidence, connection, and credibility. When someone asks a question—acknowledge it with respect, then respond directly.

5. **Be rooted in authenticity.**
   Don't try to impress—aim to connect. Speak from your truth. Let your energy reflect your message. When your passion is real, your audience can feel it.

6. **Rehearse—but don't memorize.**

   Practice your key points until they're comfortable, but don't script every word. A compelling speaker sounds natural, not robotic. Your goal isn't perfection—it's presence.

7. **Record and review.**

   Use your phone to record yourself. Play it back and reflect. Are you convincing? Are you confident? Are you compelling? Adjust as needed—then try again.

Every step you take toward being more compelling is a step toward greater influence and impact. Embrace the process, learn from each interaction, and let your confidence grow. You have what it takes to captivate and inspire.

## Final Roar

Being compelling isn't about being the loudest voice in the room—it's about being the clearest, the most grounded, and the most real.

When you speak with truth, passion, and purpose, you become magnetic—not because you're trying to impress, but because you're rooted in conviction.

Whether you're pitching an idea, sharing your story, or standing up for what matters, remember:

You have the power to influence.

You have the presence to inspire.

You have a voice that deserves to be heard.

*Let your inner lioness roar—*
*with clarity, with purpose,*
*and with conviction.*

# Visionary

## What It Means to Be Visionary

The word visionary stems from the Latin *visionarius*, meaning "of seeing" or "having foresight." And to be honest, I love everything about this word. It doesn't just describe someone with big dreams—it captures the essence of someone who can see beyond what's in front of them. Someone who can look past the obstacles, the chaos, the noise, and the now, and instead imagine what could be.

When I think of a visionary, I think of someone with a strategic mindset—who can see the forest for the trees. Visionaries can think outside the box and consider unconventional paths to solve problems. They don't just operate on autopilot; they pause, assess, and explore alternative approaches others may overlook. While many see only one solution, the visionary sees possibilities.

But here's the thing: being visionary isn't just about having your head in the clouds. A true visionary can also get tactical when needed. They know how to help steer a team when it's stuck, structure a plan when it's falling apart, and organize chaos into clarity. They can lead from the front—not with ego, but with intention and foresight. They inspire forward momentum, especially when others lose sight of the destination.

Being visionary also doesn't have to happen on a global or corporate scale. It can be something as small and personal as planning a trip months in advance—mapping out what needs to happen to bring that experience to life. It's about having the forethought to design your days, weeks, and months with purpose and clarity. Visionaries zoom out. They don't just live in the weeds; they consciously lift their eyes to see the big picture.

*"The most dangerous phrase in the language is,*
*'We've always done it this way.'"*
—Grace Hopper

History has always been shaped by visionaries—especially women who dared to see a world that didn't yet exist. Think of Dorothy Vaughan, one of the brilliant Black women behind NASA's early space program, who led with vision and brilliance in a system that barely acknowledged her presence. Her story, brought to life by Octavia Spencer in *Hidden Figures*, reminds us that visionaries often work in silence, pushing boundaries before the world is ready to recognize them.

Stories like hers aren't just inspiring—they're a call to action. That visionary fire is still needed today, because the systems we're navigating haven't caught up. For all the progress we've made, too many of us still find ourselves bumping up against old systems built without us in mind—systems that weren't designed to make space for our voices, our brilliance, or our leadership.

For example, the "Good Old Boys Club" might not always wear a name badge anymore, but its influence still lingers. It shapes a culture of exclusivity where access and advancement are often reserved for insiders. This leaves many women sidelined despite their talents. If you don't think it does, pay closer attention to the women around you. Watch how meetings unfold— notice who gets interrupted, overlooked, or left out of opportunities. When you begin to see it, you can no longer unsee it.

And dismantling it doesn't always happen with a loud crash—nor through the grit and determination of a single woman. Sometimes, it's the quiet persistence of showing up, claiming space, and refusing to play small.

It's in the way we rise, again and again, even when the odds are stacked against us.

It's in the moments we speak up—not just for ourselves, but for others.

And it's in the echo of our collective roar—women lifting each other, rewriting the rules, and refusing to let outdated systems define our worth or limit our leadership.

That same visionary energy is what led me to dream bigger than just a book. *Roar Like A Woman* isn't just a title—it's the beginning of a movement. A call to action. A philosophy born from this belief:

> **When women unleash their inner lioness,**
> **they create ripples of transformation**
> **that extend far beyond themselves.**

I don't just want to write about empowerment—I want to ignite it. I see a world where women stand in their truth, speak with power, and rise together—and I want this platform, this message, and this community to lead that change. I've decided to build a movement, to become a bold and visible voice, and to create space for women everywhere to roar unapologetically.

**And if you're holding this book in your hands, you're already part of that vision.**

Being visionary takes a shift in mindset. It's about approaching your life with curiosity and openness, not perfection. It's about lifting your gaze from the grind of daily tasks and daring to ask: *Where do I want this to go?* And then, taking action. You don't have to have all the answers. You just need to be willing to ask bold questions, see beyond today, and give yourself grace when the outcome isn't perfect.

Be visionary in your daily, weekly, and monthly goals. Start seeing your life not just as a series of tasks, but as a living roadmap you are creating. Over time, you'll start to feel the shift—not just in your perspective, but in your power.

## Are You Holding Yourself Back?

Have you ever caught yourself saying, "I'm just not a big-picture thinker" or "That's too far down the road to worry about right now?" If so, you're not alone—but you may be unintentionally limiting your ability to be visionary.

Sometimes we get so caught up in the day-to-day whirlwind of tasks, responsibilities, and reacting to what's right in front of us that we lose sight of the bigger picture. We trade foresight for fire-fighting. We focus so much on what's urgent that we forget to prioritize what's important.

Being visionary doesn't mean you must predict the future or craft a master plan for your life in one sitting. It means intentionally choosing to pause, zoom out, and consider what direction you're heading before you get too far off course. And yes, it requires mental discipline. It's easier to stay in the comfort of the present moment than to step into the unknown and imagine something greater.

We may also hold ourselves back because we think we need all the answers before we can lead with vision. But that's just not true. Being visionary isn't about having certainty—it's about having clarity of intention and the willingness to explore possibilities, even if you don't have it all figured out yet.

You might be holding yourself back if:

- You struggle to plan beyond the immediate future.
- You find yourself saying: "That's just how it's always been done."
- You fear failure so much that you avoid taking bold leaps.
- You're waiting for permission instead of trusting your intuition.

If any of that sounds familiar, don't worry—you're not stuck. You're simply being invited to shift your mindset and stretch your perspective. Embracing a visionary mindset is not just a choice. It's a powerful tool for personal growth and empowerment.

*It's time to start seeing*
*beyond the immediate tasks*
*and boldly envision*
*the life you truly want.*

## Building the Skill: How to Strengthen Your Visionary Mindset

Visionary thinking is like a lens—the more you adjust it, the clearer your future becomes. Here are some ways to start developing your visionary mindset:

1. **Practice future-casting.**
   Set aside time each week to ask yourself big-picture questions: Where do I want to be in six months? One year? What kind of life am I designing for myself? Don't worry about having perfect answers—just start exploring the possibilities.

2. **Create a vision journal or a vision board.**
   Dedicate a space where you can freely dream and brainstorm ideas, both personal and professional. Include sketches, mind maps, travel plans, business ideas—anything that sparks your imagination. Permit yourself to dream without judgment.

3. **Zoom out before you zoom in.**
   Before tackling your to-do list each day, pause to consider: How does this fit into the larger picture of what I'm trying to build? This small habit helps ensure your daily actions align with your long-term vision.

4. **Challenge conventional thinking.**
   Next time you're stuck on a problem, ask: What's another way? What haven't we tried yet? Explore non-traditional paths. Visionaries often find solutions in the places others overlook.

5. **Surround yourself with forward-thinking people.**

Seek conversations with people who inspire and challenge you. Vision is contagious—when you surround yourself with expansive thinkers, you'll naturally start expanding your own perspective.

6. **Use micro-visions.**

Being visionary isn't reserved for large-scale movements. Practice creating "micro-visions" for your week, next project, or next vacation. Look ahead and intentionally map the steps that get you there.

7. **Give yourself grace.**

Visionary thinking doesn't mean everything will go according to plan. Be kind to yourself when the path shifts or when your vision needs refining. Flexibility is a strength, not a flaw.

> *"If your dream only includes you,*
> *it's too small."*
> —Ava DuVernay

# Final Roar

You don't need a crystal ball to be a visionary—you just need clarity, courage, and the willingness to see beyond the present moment and into the future you're meant to create.

> ***Every time you pause to reflect,***
> ***to dream, to design your path forward,***
> ***you are claiming your power as a visionary.***

Don't wait for permission. Don't shrink your perspective to fit the moment. Raise your gaze. Expand your thinking.
Lead your life with intention, and let your vision pull you forward.

# Purposeful

## What It Means to Be Purposeful

I don't live my life on autopilot. I don't wait for clarity to find me—I create it. Every decision I make, every word I speak, and every opportunity I pursue is fueled by intention. I believe in living on purpose, not by accident. Because when you've faced your own mortality, you stop waiting for someday. You start living today—with meaning, with fire, and with a deep knowing that your time is precious.

The word purposeful comes from the Latin *propositum*, meaning "a thing proposed or intended." To be purposeful means more than having a plan—it means aligning your actions with your values, your energy with your goals, and your life with your deeper why.

When I was diagnosed with breast cancer, I thought my life was over. I knew so many people who hadn't survived the disease, and it terrified me that I might become the next statistic. But like everything I do in life, I tackled that diagnosis head-on. I built a plan to kick cancer to the curb—and I followed it with determination.

And I *did* kick it to the curb. But not without acquiring new scars, not without tears, and not without a profound transformation that changed how I live forever.

As I write this book today, I'm celebrating ten years as a survivor. A decade. A full second chance at life. And because of that second chance, I made a choice: I would live #*WithPurpose*, not passivity. Although my diagnosis doesn't define me, it absolutely shaped me. That experience—painful and terrifying as it was—refined who I am at my core. It's a testament to the transformative power of personal experiences and a reminder that even the most challenging times can lead to growth and self-discovery.

During that chapter of my life, I interviewed with the American Cancer Society. I had prepared pages of notes for the interview, including carefully crafted responses, key messages, and sound bites. But somewhere midway through the interview, I abandoned the script.

Instead, I found myself speaking from the heart—about my parents, about how they raised me to be strong, independent, and proactive. About how those roots—combined with the crucible of cancer—crystallized something I now know to be my truth: *Everything I do is with purpose.*

Every word I speak, every decision I make, every opportunity I pursue—I do it with intent. I now live my life as someone who acts on everything *#WithPurpose.* That's not just a hashtag I use; it's a mantra I live by. It's in the name of my publishing company, *Act With Purpose Publishing*, and the title of my first instrumental CD, *With Purpose.* It is the very essence of who I now am.

My life is a constant evolution of seeking out opportunities to live and lead intentionally. I don't waste time. I don't wait around for life to happen to me. I move forward with clarity, vision, and direction.

And you can too. Because when life tries to take you out—and you push back and win—it forever sharpens your clarity on what truly matters.

You stop wasting time.

You stop waiting for permission.

You start living like your life depends on it.

Because it does.

*Don't wait for a crisis to wake you up—*
*claim your power and live purposefully now.*

## Are You Holding Yourself Back?

Purposeful living doesn't require a life-altering experience like a cancer diagnosis, but it does demand reflection. Many of us live in reactive mode—responding to the demands of the day, the needs of others, or the pull of convenience. Without realizing it, we drift.

Ask yourself:

- Are you moving through life with clear intent, or are you simply going through the motions?
- Do your daily choices align with your bigger goals and values?
- When you say "yes" to something, are you doing it because it matters, or because it's expected or easier?

If you nodded yes to any of those questions, you're not alone. Sometimes, we're afraid to define a clear purpose because it means setting boundaries, saying "no", or acknowledging that some things no longer serve us.

And that's a hard realization to come to grips with. It can challenge the very foundation of how we were raised—especially if we were taught to be everything to everyone. I could write an entire book on boundaries alone, because saying no often feels like letting people down, even ourselves. But without boundaries, living with purpose becomes almost impossible.

But clarity is power.

And living life with intent means making decisions congruent with who you are—and who you're becoming, not who others expect you to be.

*You're not here*
*to live someone else's version of your life.*
*It's yours to define.*

# Building the Skill: Living With Purpose

Purpose isn't a finish line—it's a way of living. Below are some of the ways I practice living purposefully every day, and how you can begin doing the same:

1. **Define what matters most.**
   Take time to articulate your core values. What truly matters to you? What do you want to be known for? When you know your "why," the "what" becomes easier to navigate. Remember, your "why" might evolve—and that's okay. Mine shifted this year, and the result is the book you're holding in your hands.

2. **Start each day with intention.**
   Whether it's through journaling, setting daily intentions, or repeating a personal mantra, begin each day with a moment of grounded focus. Don't let the day hijack you—claim it.

3. **Reflect often.**
   Establish a weekly ritual to pause and reflect on your actions. Are you spending time where it counts? Are you investing in what energizes and fulfills you?

4. **Say "no" more often.**
   Purposeful living requires pruning. Say "no" to things that don't align with your values, goals, or energy. Saying "no" to one thing means saying "yes" to something better.

5. **Act #WithPurpose—always.**
   This doesn't mean over-planning or being rigid. It means choosing to act, speak, and live in alignment with your morals, values, and essence. You don't have to wait for the perfect moment. You just need to be clear, consistent, and intentional.

6. **Create a purpose statement.**
   Write a personal statement that defines how you want to live and lead. Post it where you can see it daily. Let it become your compass.

Purpose is a practice, not a destination. You don't need to overhaul your entire life in one leap. Just start with one choice—one moment—and do it with intention. Purpose builds momentum. And the more you live with it, the more powerful and fulfilled you'll feel.

## Final Roar

**You are not lost.**

You are choosing your path—with intention, with courage, and with fire.

Every decision, every step, every breath is an opportunity to live deliberately.

The world needs more women who lead with grounded strength—women who know their worth and act from a place of truth and self-trust.

When you commit to living purposefully, you're not just changing your own life—you're shaping a legacy. You're becoming a lighthouse in someone else's storm.

**Because purpose isn't a finish line.**

It's a force.

It's the steady rhythm that guides your "yes" and fortifies your "no".

It's the reason you rise in the morning—and the legacy you leave behind.

**You are not here to drift.**

You are here to decide.

To direct your energy with clarity,

to move with meaning,

to light the path for others who are still finding their way.

**So keep showing up.**

**Keep choosing alignment.**

**Keep living with purpose and intent.**

*And never forget:*

Your life is not random.

It is **rooted**.

It is **ready**.

It is **roaring** with meaning.

# Waymaker

## What It Means to Be a Waymaker

A Waymaker isn't someone who shouts the loudest or seeks the spotlight. She's the one who walks beside you when the path is uncertain—clearing space, offering wisdom, and helping you rise with quiet strength and unwavering support. She doesn't just open doors; she hands you the key and reminds you you've had it all along.

History is filled with quiet Waymakers—women whose names you may never read in textbooks, but whose impact shaped generations. Think of Harriet Tubman, who risked her life again and again to lead others to freedom. Or Dolores Huerta, who organized farmworkers with tireless resolve and coined the rallying cry "Sí se puede." These women didn't wait for an invitation. They saw injustice and carved a path toward something better—not for recognition, but for liberation. Their power came not from position, but from purpose.

While their paths were etched into history, Waymakers still walk among us—often unnoticed, but no less powerful. I met one early in my career.

I had just stepped into a new role that placed me at the forefront of our sales process—traveling to client sites, delivering high-stakes software demonstrations, and representing our company in rooms full of decision-makers. I had experience, but not in this exact arena. I knew I had to bring my absolute best—but I wasn't quite sure what that would look like.

That's when one of my colleagues—a seasoned, sharp, and quietly brilliant woman—took me under her wing. Officially, she was just training me. But what she actually did was mentor me.

She taught me how to pitch—not just the product, but the potential. How to amplify the software's best features and confidently speak to our customization capabilities. She helped me find the rhythm of a strong sales narrative and taught me how to hold my ground when tough questions arose.

And then she went deeper—teaching me how to read a room, how to speak the language of executives without minimizing my voice, and how to navigate the all-too-familiar boardroom dynamics that come when you're the only woman presenting to a room full of men.

She instilled in me the importance of respecting myself in every interaction. She reminded me that knowledge is powerful when paired with humility. She showed me how to physically lean into a conversation when others start to pull back.

She even offered travel hacks—how to pack smart, how to stay poised during flight delays, and how to walk into a client meeting looking like you'd just had ten hours of sleep... even when you only had two.

She didn't just prepare me for the job—she prepared me to show up fully as myself. That's what Waymakers do. They don't simply lead from the front. They walk beside us until we're strong enough to lead, too.

And now, that's the kind of Waymaker I strive to be. I believe that *Roar Like A Woman* isn't just about our individual journeys—it's about what happens when we rise and bring others with us. When we show up with our confident roar, we give silent permission for the women around us to do the same. Our voice becomes a spark. Our courage becomes contagious.

Every woman has an inner lioness inside her. Sometimes she just needs to be reminded she's allowed to roar. When we walk in our truth, speak with conviction, and shine without apology, we light the way for others to follow. That's the power of being a Waymaker—not in blazing glory, but in steady, intentional presence. We don't just make a way forward—we *invite others into it.*

## Are You Holding Yourself Back?

Being a Waymaker requires courage and vulnerability. It means showing up for others, often before you feel fully ready yourself. If you're someone who naturally helps others, you may find yourself pouring energy into everyone else's path—but forgetting to honor your own. This is something every woman needs to recognize, acknowledge, and course-correct so we don't allow our roar to be diminished.

Ask yourself the following:

- Are you offering support to others without asking for help in return?
- Are you afraid to claim the title of "leader" or "mentor" because you don't think you've "earned it" yet?
- Do you intentionally dim your own light while lighting the path for others?

Sometimes we hold ourselves back from being Waymakers because we feel unqualified. We doubt whether our perspective, experiences, or story can truly make a difference. But the truth is, you don't have to have all the answers. You just have to be *willing* to walk beside someone, ask thoughtful questions, and believe in their ability to grow and develop.

A Waymaker is someone who clears the brush, shines a light, or walks quietly beside someone else until they feel strong enough to walk alone. If you're holding yourself back because you're waiting for a title, permission, or perfection—you're missing the truth: *You already are* someone who can change lives.

# Building the Skill: How to Embrace Being a Waymaker

Becoming a Waymaker isn't about waiting until you feel fully prepared—it's about starting with what you already have: your voice, your heart, your story, and your willingness to support others. These strategies are designed to help you step more confidently into your role as a guide, mentor, and quiet force for change. Your influence matters, whether you're leading from the front or walking beside someone in silence.

1. **Identify your natural gifts as a helper or guide.**
   What comes naturally to you? Do people often seek your advice, ask for your input, or feel comforted in your presence? Take note of where you have already made a difference.

2. **Mentor with intention.**
   Find someone in your circle—at work, in your community, or even in your family—and offer consistent, thoughtful support. You don't have to solve their problems, but you can ask empowering questions to help them think through solutions.

3. **Use reflective listening to help others gain clarity.**
   Sometimes the greatest gift you can give someone is your full attention. Practice listening not to respond, but to understand. Let your presence help them organize their thoughts and see the road ahead.

4. **Don't be afraid to challenge limiting beliefs.**
   As a Waymaker, part of your role is to help others break free from the mental constraints holding them back. Gently challenge their assumptions with empathy and encourage them to let go of limiting beliefs.

5. **Make space for your own path.**
   Helping others is powerful, but not at the expense of your own growth. Prioritize your goals and allow others to support you as well. You can't lead with clarity if your own vision is cloudy.

6. **Share your story.**

   Your journey—complete with obstacles, detours, and triumphs—is a roadmap for someone else. Don't be afraid to open up. You never know whose way you're making just by speaking your truth.

7. **Embrace your purpose.**

   Let your desire to help others be anchored in your own sense of meaning. Whether through conversation, coaching, community, or quiet guidance, remind yourself often: *This is why I'm here.*

Every time you speak up, advocate for someone, or create space for another woman to rise—you're not just helping in that moment. You're contributing to a movement. *Roar Like A Woman* was born from that spirit of everyday courage, and it belongs to all of us who choose to lead with heart.

When you do, you're following in the footsteps of powerful, resilient women who came before you—those who spoke truth to power, lifted others as they rose, and dared to believe in a world where every voice matters. Their legacy lives on in you.

*Every small act of courage becomes part of the roar.*

## Final Roar

Being a Waymaker isn't about having all the answers—it's about being brave enough to go first, kind enough to walk with others, and wise enough to step aside when they're ready to lead.

*I carry the torch*
*so others can see their way forward.*
*That's what it means to Roar Like A Woman.*

I am a Waymaker.

I clear paths, light the way, and walk beside others with intention and care.

My purpose is powerful.

My presence makes a difference.

My story helps others rise.

I lead with heart, and I empower with grace.

# Transforming

## What Does It Mean to Be Transforming?

Transforming is not just about surface-level change—it's about evolution with intention. It is the courageous, ongoing process of becoming a more empowered and authentic version of yourself. It means shedding outdated roles, limiting beliefs, or external expectations and boldly stepping into who you are meant to be—with clarity, purpose, and fierce self-acceptance.

From the Latin *transformare*, meaning "to change in shape or form," the word reminds us that transformation is rarely comfortable—but always powerful.

Transformation is deeply personal, yet it often becomes the catalyst for an impact that extends beyond ourselves. When we transform, we don't just change—we become capable of leading, inspiring, mentoring, and empowering others through the example of our own growth.

Transforming can look like many things:

- A woman returning to school after raising her children, and rediscovering her sense of purpose.
- A leader learning to listen more deeply and lead with empathy.
- A survivor rewriting her story with strength instead of shame.
- Someone leaving a job, relationship, or mindset that no longer fits—and choosing themselves instead.

As part of the journey to unleash your inner lioness, transformation is essential.

*It's not about waiting*
*for life to change you—*
*it's about choosing*
*to evolve yourself, on purpose.*

Between September 2024 and May 2025, I made that choice. I committed to a season of intentional growth. I asked myself, "Who do I want to become next?" and then got to work. I picked up leadership and self-development books and immersed myself in the tools that would help me reconnect with my values and amplify my strengths.

One of the most powerful tools I found was journaling. Julia Cameron's *The Artist's Way* introduced me to the practice of Morning Pages—three pages of handwritten, stream-of-consciousness writing every morning. These pages cleared my mind, calmed my inner critic, and gave voice to the truths that had been hiding beneath the surface.

Cameron also encourages weekly Artist Dates—solo creative outings that nourish your spirit and curiosity. Whether it was walking through a local art fair, browsing books, or simply sitting alone with coffee and a notebook, these weekly dates helped reconnect me with myself.

I also began a nightly ritual of writing 3–5 affirmations or manifestations before bed. I would revisit them each morning and reflect on them as I wrote in my Morning Pages. That combination—evening intention and morning clarity—became a framework for my personal transformation. Through this practice, I discovered that my passion is helping others uncover and amplify their own worth. I don't want just to share stories—I want to equip, inspire, and uplift. And that's how *Roar Like A Woman* was born.

Although I began working on this book in March 2024, it wasn't until February 2025—after months of reading, writing, reflecting, and becoming—that the whole vision for this book came into focus. It was not a moment of magic. It was the result of transformation. Finally, in May 2025, my inner artist was unleashed. I found clarity to write the raw, vulnerable, and fundamental truths that you are now reading.

Your transformation might look different than mine. And that's precisely the point—it's supposed to.

And here's what I now know for sure: meaningful transformation takes work and requires effort. But when you *show up for yourself*—day after day—with intention and self-compassion, you begin to unlock something powerful. You start to see yourself not just as someone changing—but as someone becoming. Becoming wiser. Braver. Louder. *Intentional.* Softer. More you.

When you do that—when you choose transformation over standing still—you don't just grow for yourself. You grow to lead, to guide, and to impact others. That is the power of transformation. That's the ripple effect that creates a movement. That's how you unleash the soulful roar of your inner lioness.

## Are You Holding Yourself Back?

Transformation can be both thrilling and terrifying at the same time. Sometimes, the idea of becoming the next version of yourself is less scary than the idea of letting go of the current version. We get attached to our titles, our roles, our routines—even our fears.

> *But holding on*
> *to who you've been*
> *can quietly hold you back*
> *from who you're meant to be.*

Ask yourself honestly:

- Are you clinging to outdated definitions of success, identity, or worthiness that no longer reflect who you are?
- Do you fear that if you change, people won't understand you—or worse, that you'll lose relationships built on the "old you"?

- Are you waiting for permission, the "right" moment, or some form of external validation to begin your transformation?
- Do you stop yourself from dreaming bigger because you think it's too late, too hard, or not realistic?

Let me be clear: Transformation doesn't require perfection—it requires presence. And sometimes the biggest shift comes not from doing more, but from releasing what no longer fits.

You might be holding yourself back if you:

- Talk yourself out of what you really want, convincing yourself to settle for less.
- Say yes to things that drain you, just to avoid disappointing others.
- Resist change because you're afraid you won't recognize the person on the other side.

But here's the truth: you are allowed to evolve. You are meant to.

*And the moment you decide*
*to stop standing in your own way*
*is the moment*
*transformation begins.*

## Building the Skill: Embrace the Power of Transforming

Transformation is a marathon, not a sprint. It requires time, patience, and a commitment to yourself. These strategies are meant to help you build momentum toward your next empowered self:

1. **Define your next chapter.**
   Ask yourself: *What does the next version of me look like? How does she think, lead, speak, and live?* Write it down. Describe her in vivid detail. Once you can see her clearly, you'll begin to move toward her.

2. **Try Morning Pages and Artist Dates.**

   Start with a week of Morning Pages—three pages of handwritten journaling, first thing in the morning. If three pages seem overwhelming,
   then commit to writing one or two. Just do something. Don't censor
   yourself. Let your thoughts, fears, and dreams spill out. Pair this with a
   weekly Artist Date—an hour alone doing something joyful or inspiring.
   You'll be amazed at the insight this duo unlocks.

3. **Start a manifestation or affirmation journal.**

   Each night, write 3–5 "I am" statements or desires you're calling into
   your life. These should feel exciting, empowering, and aligned with
   your growth. Review them each morning to refocus your energy and
   intentions.

4. **Identify one thing you're ready to release.**

   Transformation often starts with letting go. Is it a toxic habit? A limiting
   belief? A relationship that no longer aligns? Write it down. Say it out
   loud. And choose one small action to begin releasing it.

5. **Surround yourself with expansion.**

   Join a group, community, or network that stretches you. Read books,
   listen to podcasts, or follow voices that challenge you to think bigger
   and act braver. If your circle isn't growing with you, it might be time to
   expand your circle.

6. **Build in pause and reflection.**

   Transformation doesn't happen when you're racing on autopilot. Set
   aside time each week to pause and reflect. Ask: *How am I evolving?*
   *What's feeling aligned? What needs to shift?* Insight follows intention.

Transformation isn't about becoming someone else—it's about returning
to the most powerful, aligned version of who you've always been. These
practices aren't just tools; they're invitations to reconnect with yourself,
to grow with intention, and to rise with clarity. Give yourself the grace to
evolve at your own pace. Trust that every small step is reshaping your path,
expanding your purpose, and building the life you're here to live.

## Final Roar

Transformation is not a destination—it's a lifelong journey of growth, awareness, and intentional evolution.

The woman you are today is not the final version of you.

Every day offers an opportunity to refine your vision, release what no longer serves you, and move closer to your truth.

You are not just transforming for yourself—you are transforming #With-Purpose.

*Transformation is a process of becoming, not arriving.*
*And I am becoming more of myself each day.*

When you embrace the process of becoming—with grace, courage, and deliberate intention—you don't just change your life.

You create a ripple that wakes others up to their own power.

And that is how transformation becomes a movement.

# Thriving

## What It Means to Thrive

Thriving isn't just about success—it's about energy. Motion. Momentum. When I think of someone who's thriving, I don't picture someone sitting still, satisfied with the status quo. I picture someone in full motion: juggling multiple projects, ideas, roles, and responsibilities—with a fire in their eyes and a radiant joy in their stride.

The word thriving comes from the Old Norse *thrīfan*, which means "to flourish, grow vigorously, or prosper." And that's exactly how I experience it—thriving feels like personal growth in fast-forward, like everything is blooming at once. For most of my life, I've associated it with hustle: the women who seem to have endless side gigs, creative outlets, full-time jobs, and passion projects. They weren't overwhelmed—they were lit up and constantly moving.

To me, thriving is a rhythm, a harmony of passion and productivity. It's the feeling of being in your element and then amplifying that into something empowering and magnetic.

When I feel like I'm truly thriving, it's never during rest (although rest is necessary and sacred). It's when I'm all in—firing on all cylinders. I'm writing, crafting, mentoring, leading at work, and brainstorming the next big idea—sometimes all in the same week. I feel alive, aligned, and inspired. And when that kind of energy flows through me, confidence follows. New ideas flow more freely. People are drawn in, inspired by the energy, and often find themselves stepping up their own game.

Thriving, as it turns out, is contagious.

But I've also learned that thriving—when unchecked—can edge danger-ously close to burnout.

After being diagnosed with breast cancer, I found myself saying "yes" to everything that felt meaningful. I became a *Portrait of Hope* for the American Cancer Society, attended events, gave speeches, and mentally prepared for each engagement. I was honored as a *Torchlighter* for United Way, wrote songs for my *With Purpose* CD, and kept up with a full-time job that demanded my best every day. On the outside, I looked like I was thriving. On the inside, I was still healing—from surgeries, from trauma, from the invisible weight of fear of recurrence.

What most people didn't see was that during all of this, I was still going back every three months for post-cancer checkups. Because I'd had a double mastectomy, I no longer had enough breast tissue for mammograms—so the only way to check for recurrence was through physical exams and scans. I didn't realize it at the time, but as each appointment approached, my stress and anxiety quietly built. I'd start snapping at people, crying over small things, feeling this tightening in my chest I couldn't explain.

Then the appointment would come. I'd hear the words—"Everything looks good. No evidence of disease."—and I would dissolve. Sometimes in my car. Sometimes in the bathroom at work. I thought I was thriving. But I was also holding my breath, over and over again, waiting for the relief that I was still okay.

That pattern became its own kind of emotional whiplash—high achieve-ment on the outside, silent survival on the inside. I had poured myself into purpose, into productivity, into saying "yes" to everything that gave me meaning—but I hadn't left space for release. Or rest. Or repair. I had confused thriving with convincing myself I was okay, not just proving it to others. And the truth is, I was still trying to feel safe and whole in my own body.

It took time—and honesty—to realize that thriving doesn't mean saying yes to everything that gives you purpose. It means creating space for joy, not crowding it out. Thriving should feel energizing, not depleting.

There's a beauty in how thriving allows us to elevate not just ourselves, but the people around us. When you're living in that state—when you're in sync with your strengths, your creativity, and your drive—you become a force of encouragement for others. You raise the energetic bar. You inspire others to match your momentum, and together, you co-create a culture of growth and development.

Thriving isn't about perfection or productivity for productivity's sake. It's about being deeply connected to your purpose and passions, and letting that flow into everything you touch.

## Are You Holding Yourself Back?

Thriving can be an exhilarating feeling—until we start questioning whether we "deserve" it, or if we can keep up with the pace we've set for ourselves. As women, we often walk the tightrope between thriving and burning out. And sometimes, we unconsciously sabotage our own thriving energy because we've internalized a belief that too much joy, too much success, or too much ambition must be dimmed to make others comfortable.

So we downplay our wins to keep things easy for others. We may hit pause on our momentum because we worry we'll lose balance. Or worse, we confuse thriving with overachieving, and guilt creeps in when we're not doing everything at once.

You might be holding yourself back from thriving if:

- You feel guilty or selfish when you prioritize your own goals or creative projects.
- You tell yourself: *I'll get back to me after I finish everything for everyone else.*
- You fear that you'll attract judgment or resentment if you shine too brightly.
- You stop yourself from starting something new because you worry you can't sustain it long-term.

Here's the truth: Thriving doesn't mean you have to hustle until you collapse. Thriving means aligning your time, energy, and purpose so that you feel alive, empowered, and expansive. You don't have to earn that energy through exhaustion. You just have to give yourself permission to live in your fullest expression.

## Building the Skill: Strategies to Help You Thrive

Thriving is more than just managing a busy calendar—it's about fueling your life with clarity, joy, and alignment. Here are some practical strategies to help you tap into your thriving energy and sustain it in healthy, meaningful ways:

1. **Identify what lights you up.**
   Take inventory of the projects, people, and passions that energize you. Write them down. The more you align your time with what fuels you, the more naturally you'll thrive.

2. **Design your thrive zone.**
   Create a physical or mental space that supports your energy. This could be a creative nook, a motivating playlist, a color-coded planner, or even a vision board that reminds you of your "why."

3. **Practice momentum mapping.**
   Break your big goals or projects into mini wins. Use a daily or weekly system (even Post-it Notes!) to check things off and track your progress. Small victories fuel the thriving engine.

4. **Say yes (to you).**
   Say "yes" to opportunities that stretch and excite you. Say "yes" to collaboration. Say "yes" to visibility. Most importantly, say "yes" to yourself before saying "yes" to everyone else.

5. **Guard your energy.**
   Thriving requires boundaries. Protect your time from energy-drainers. Delegate when needed. Learn to say "no" without guilt—especially when a "yes" would come at the cost of your well-being.

6. **Celebrate out loud.**

   Don't just survive the week—celebrate the wins. Share your joy, your progress, and your breakthroughs with your circle. Thriving is contagious, and your light gives others permission to shine too.

7. **Check in often.**

   Thriving isn't a one-time achievement—it's an ongoing state. Ask yourself weekly: Am I feeling expansive or constricted? Energized or drained? Aligned or off-track? Use these reflections to recalibrate and make course corrections.

When you allow yourself to thrive, you become a living example of what's possible. Your energy becomes a spark—igniting progress, creativity, and confidence in yourself and others.

## Final Roar

Thriving isn't a finish line—it's a way of being.

It's when your purpose, your energy, and your passions align so powerfully that you can't help but radiate inspiration. When you thrive, you don't just elevate your own life—you uplift everyone around you. You become the spark that lights up the room, the idea that launches a movement, the presence that permits others to grow. It's a journey that's worth every step.

*You are not here to play small,*
*shrink down,*
*or wait your turn.*
*You are here to thrive—*
*and set the standard*
*for what's possible.*

# V

# Awaken Curiosity

# Learning, Discovery, and Expression

The final part of this journey is about opening up—to new ideas, new perspectives, and new ways of experiencing the world and yourself. Curiosity is where growth begins. It's what keeps your spirit alive, your mind sharp, and your voice vibrant. The themes you'll explore in Part V center around words like *Inquisitive, Insightful, Empathetic,* and *Thoughtful.* These empowering words invite you to become a lifelong learner and a more intentional, emboldened communicator.

Women are often encouraged to be agreeable instead of inquisitive. But let's reframe that. Curiosity is not rebellion—it's wisdom in motion. It's the power to ask better questions, to challenge outdated narratives, and to wonder what else might be possible.

*It's not just about being curious,*
*it's about being empowered by your curiosity*
*so you can grow*
*into an even more empowered and*
*evolved version of yourself.*

When we allow ourselves to explore, we discover truths we didn't know we were seeking. We give ourselves the freedom to evolve, express ourselves, and fully engage with the world around us. Curiosity connects us to each other and to ourselves.

This section is about giving yourself permission to be curious without needing to have all the answers. It's about letting discovery lead the way and trusting that your voice is powerful, even when it's still forming.

Let these words reawaken your sense of wonder. Let them inspire your questions, your growth, and your bold self-expression.

The journey doesn't end here—this is just the beginning.

Stay curious. Stay open. Keep growing.

# Inquisitive

## What It Means to Be Inquisitive

The Latin root of inquisitive comes from *inquirere*—"to seek after, to search deeply." And while we often think of being inquisitive as exploring the outside world, some of the most transformational questions we'll ever ask are the ones we direct inward.

*Who am I becoming?*

*What matters most to me?*

*What am I afraid to see?*

Being inquisitive isn't just about knowing more. It's about knowing yourself more fully—and being brave enough to look, even when the answers might shake you.

My first language of exploration was music. I started learning piano at the age of five, taught by my mom on our upright piano in the family room. I remember my lesson books, my mom sitting beside me, showing me how to hold my hands in the proper formation, and patiently teaching me how the notes blended together to create harmony or dissonance. Then, how to shape those notes into emotional sounds that could tug on the heartstrings. I was fascinated by the process.

By the time I was 12 or 13, I decided I wanted to write my own song. I called it *On the Wings of a Dove.* I scribbled out the melody and bass lines and believed in that song so fiercely that I wanted to protect it. This was before Google (yes, it was that long ago), before online forms or templates. So I asked my parents: "How do you copyright a song?? We went to the library together and figured out the steps. I wrote a letter addressed to the U.S. Copyright Office and included all the necessary information to file a copyright for a piece of music. My dad helped me package up the handwritten score and the letter, and we sent it off in the mail.

That song is long gone—I don't even remember if I ever received a response—but the memory of my dad and me standing at the mailbox and dropping that letter officially into the mail is forever burned into my heart.

That act wasn't just about protecting a song. It was about claiming my voice. At that age, I was already asking the kind of questions that matter for inquisitive growth: *What do I want to say? How do I protect what I've created? How can I own my story before someone else tries to rewrite it?*

That spark of self-exploration stayed with me. I joined the marching band, the jazz band, and sang in church choirs. In college, I became part of an all-female vocal group called *Undivided.* That was when I discovered what it meant to be a performer—but more importantly, I began learning what it meant to express myself through art.

Even then, I wasn't content to play someone else's notes. I wanted to understand *how* music worked. What made chords clash or resolve? Why did one harmony move people to tears while another made them rise to their feet? I studied artists who played and sang simultaneously and attempted to emulate their flow, passion, and presence.

That same spirit of self-inquiry followed me into every season of life. When I entered the corporate world, I brought that same drive with me. I didn't want just to check boxes—I wanted to ask better questions. To understand people. To challenge broken systems. To create momentum that mattered.

I don't share all of these accomplishments from my youth to brag, but to share an important realization with you: it is that drive to constantly search for *more*—that never-ending desire to understand how things work, how to do more and be more to help others, how people think, what makes the world go around—that inquisitive nature is what has helped mold me into the person I am today.

And that has led me to understand something else critically essential: *we cannot guide others until we are willing to explore our own depths*—and understand how we interact with and influence the world around us.

To be inquisitive is to stay in motion. To remain open. To believe that there is always more to discover—about the world, about others, and most importantly, about yourself.

You don't need all the answers. You just need the courage to keep asking the hard, explorative questions that unveil new opportunities to discover more.

## Are You Holding Yourself Back?

It's easy to associate being inquisitive with exploring the outside world—books, ideas, systems, and other people. But some of the most difficult and courageous questions we'll ever ask are the ones we direct inward.

*Why do I react this way?*

*What am I really afraid of?*

*What patterns am I repeating—and why?*

Yet somewhere along the way, many of us learned to quiet those questions. Maybe we were told not to rock the boat. Perhaps we feared what we might uncover. Maybe self-exploration felt too uncomfortable, too indulgent, or too uncertain.

- Have you ever ignored your own instincts because digging deeper felt too risky?
- Have you ever avoided journaling or reflection because you didn't want to "go there"?
- Have you ever felt the pull of growth, but chosen safety instead?

If so, you're not alone. And you're not broken. You're human.

But here's what I know for sure: the women who lead with clarity are the ones who've learned to sit with themselves, in their own vulnerability and truth. They've asked the hard personal questions. They've let the silence speak. And they've dared to get inquisitive—not just about the world, but about their own soul.

By exploring your own thoughts, patterns, and inner wiring—how you think, how you process, what drives you—you begin to build inquisitive strength. This strength empowers your ability to connect with, understand, and influence others in a more authentic, empathetical and impactful way.

You may be holding yourself back if:

- You avoid self-reflection because it feels overwhelming or pointless.
- You crave change but don't know where to start, so you stay stuck.
- You resist asking "why" because you're afraid of the answer.
- You dismiss your own questions as silly, dramatic, or too big to solve.
- You're constantly seeking answers from others, but rarely pause to ask yourself.

Being inquisitive isn't just a sign of intelligence. It's a sign of self-trust. The moment you start asking more in-depth questions—of yourself, *for yourself*—is the moment you start moving.

## Building the Skill: How to Cultivate Inquisitiveness

Being inquisitive isn't just about seeking answers—it's about being brave enough to ask the tough questions—especially your own.

It's easy to get caught up in collecting facts or chasing knowledge for the sake of being "in the know." But true introspective inquiry—the kind that transforms you—asks you to turn inward first. To explore the stories you've told yourself. To examine what you've inherited, absorbed, accepted, or believed without question.

You don't need to know everything. You just need to be willing to ask: *What else might be true?*

Here are some intentional ways to cultivate a curious, open, and self-aware mindset:

1. **Ask yourself better questions.**

   Instead of *What's wrong with me?* ask, *What might I need right now?* Instead of *Why can't I figure this out?* try, *What else might be possible?* Shifting your questions softens your inner voice and opens new mental doors.

2. **Create a curiosity ritual.**

   Spend 10 minutes a day journaling or walking without distraction. Use the time to check in: *What's pulling at me today? What am I avoiding? What do I need to explore emotionally, creatively, or spiritually?*

3. **Listen to your resistance.**

   When something triggers discomfort or defensiveness, pause. Ask: *Why is this bothering me? What belief is this bumping up against?* Inquisitiveness turns resistance into insight.

4. **Practice present-moment noticing.**

   Awareness thrives in the now. Tune into how your body responds to specific environments, people, or decisions. Let attention—not judgment—guide what you learn.

5. **Stay open to change.**

   Being inquisitive means being open to evolving your beliefs. If something you once believed no longer fits, you don't have to defend it. You get to explore what might fit better now.

6. **Ask others meaningful questions.**

   Deep conversations begin with inquiry, not performance. Try asking people: "What's lighting you up these days?" or "What's something you're learning about yourself?" These questions invite depth and connection.

7. **Create space for silence.**

   Some of your most powerful questions will only surface in quiet moments. Make time to be still. Let the question rise—and let the answer take its time.

When you cultivate inquisitiveness as a conscious practice, not just a personality trait, you begin to lead yourself with more intention.

*And the more clearly you see yourself,*
*the more powerfully you can guide others.*

## Final Roar

Inquisitiveness isn't a distraction. It's a guide.
It points you inward when you're looking for direction.
It nudges you to ask why, even when silence feels safer.
It keeps you growing, even when others have stopped looking.

*Being inquisitive isn't about having all the answers—*
*it's about being bold enough*
*to keep asking the questions.*

# Curious

## What It Means to Be Curious

The word curious comes from the Latin root *cura*, meaning "care" or "concern." And that's exactly what curiosity is: caring enough to want to understand. It's the quiet hunger for insight, the gentle nudge that says, *Look a little closer. Ask one more question. There's more here.*

Curiosity is how we begin to untangle old stories and discover new ones. It's how we learn—not just about the world, but about ourselves as well. Yet somewhere along the way, many of us were taught to suppress our curiosity. To stop raising our hands. To only speak when we had the "right" answer. To follow the map, not the mystery.

But here's what I've learned: curiosity is not rebellion—it's wisdom in motion. It's what keeps your spirit alive, your voice vibrant, and your vision expansive. It's the difference between performing life and participating in it.

You don't have to be a scientist or philosopher to be curious. You just have to be willing to wonder. To ask *Why? What if? Could there be more than this?* If you've ever felt a tug to learn something new, explore a different path, or challenge the status quo—you already know what it means to be curious.

When I was diagnosed with breast cancer, my curiosity became my anchor. I did the one thing everyone told me not to do: I Googled it. And yes, what I found ranged from terrifying to absurd. One site recommended eating a whole bag of carrots every day as a cure. Another suggested moving to California and smoking weed. Some claimed cancer wasn't even real. None of those answers provided me with what I truly needed and what I was seeking so desperately: clarity, information, and hope.

That search made me even more curious and led me to a phone call with the American Cancer Society. A woman on the other end of the line spent 90 minutes talking me through everything—survival rates, statistics, treatment options, cancer types, support programs. Her steady voice helped calm the storm that was raging inside me. From there, I continued to ask questions. I connected with survivors. I spoke to doctors. I got second opinions. I asked more questions. I reached out to a cousin who had walked and survived this road years before.

Curiosity didn't give me certainty, but it gave me direction. And eventually, it gave me clarity and a sense of purpose. If I had this many questions—if I was searching for answers and craving the kind of hope no answer could fully provide—I knew others were, too. I realized I needed to do more. I didn't want anyone else to face the trauma, uncertainty, mortality questions, and heart-clenching fear that had shaken me to my core. So, I started volunteering. I spoke at events. I shared my story to help other women feel less afraid. That's when I truly understood that curiosity doesn't just inform you—it empowers you. And it creates that ripple effect, that quiet roar that gives others the confidence to do the same.

You don't need a grand reason to be curious. You just need to care. To listen to that whisper inside that says: *I wonder...* and follow it. Whether it leads to a new passion, a deeper understanding, or a truth you've been waiting to uncover—it's worth it.

Curiosity is how you connect. How you lead. How you grow. It's not a weakness. It's a superpower.

## Are You Holding Yourself Back?

We often outgrow our curiosity without even realizing it.

Maybe you were once the little girl who asked a million questions—but somewhere along the way, someone told you to stop. Perhaps a teacher rolled their eyes when your hand went up too often. Maybe someone called you *nosy* instead of engaged. Or you learned that the best way to succeed was to follow the rules, keep quiet, and color inside the lines.

And so you stopped asking.

In school, we're rewarded for having the "right" answer, not for asking the better question. In workplaces, we're often told to be efficient, not exploratory. And in life? Sometimes the fear of being judged, dismissed, or misunderstood is enough to keep us silent—even when we feel that deep, undeniable pull to know more.

Let's rewrite that narrative.

Curiosity isn't immaturity—it's insight. It's what allows you to evolve, connect, and lead with a fresh perspective. And in a world that often demands certainty, choosing to ask bold, open-ended questions is a radical act of empowerment.

If you found yourself nodding along to any of those examples, chances are you've developed some limiting beliefs around curiosity—beliefs we can begin to break down, together.

You may be holding yourself back if:

- You stop yourself from asking questions for fear of sounding "stupid."
- You avoid learning something new because it doesn't come easily at first.
- You silence your curiosity because it feels unproductive or inconvenient.
- You stay in your lane even when your heart is begging you to explore a new path.
- You believe you're too old, too far along, or too established to start again.

*Let your curiosity speak up again.*
*Let it interrupt your patterns.*
*Let it lead you somewhere new.*

# Building the Skill: How to Spark Curiosity

Curiosity is not just a feeling—it's a practice. It's a decision to stay open, to keep learning, and to move through life as a seeker instead of a settler. Like a flame, it needs fuel. Like any muscle, it grows stronger the more you use it.

You don't have to overhaul your life to be more curious. You just have to start paying attention to what makes you lean in, what lights you up, and what questions are quietly waiting to be asked.

Here are some intentional ways to invite more curiosity into your life:

1. **Start with one bold question.**

   Each day, ask yourself something open-ended like *What else could be true?* or *What's another way to look at this?* Write your response without judgment. Let your thoughts surprise you.

2. **Schedule an Artist Date.**

   Inspired by *The Artist's Way*, this is solo time to explore something that delights you. Visit a museum, take a walk without a plan, browse a bookstore, try a new recipe. Go somewhere that makes your brain and heart say, *Ooh, what's that?*

3. **Talk to someone outside your circle.**

   Curiosity expands when you step beyond your bubble. Reach out to someone in a completely different industry, age group, or culture. Ask them about their journey. Listen with awe.

4. **Keep a curiosity journal.**

   This can be messy, playful, or profound. Jot down questions, reflections, ideas, even things you overheard that made you pause. Let it be a space for the questions you're not ready to answer—yet. And when your heart and mind finally lean into those questions, be prepared for the explosion of curiosity's results.

5. **Learn one new thing a week.**

 A word. A tool. A mindset. A world event. Then ask: *How does this connect to the way I live, lead, or love?*

6. **Say "I don't know" with confidence.**

 It's not a sign of weakness—it's a doorway to discovery. Be the one brave enough to admit it. Then go find out.

Curiosity doesn't require a classroom or a textbook. It just needs your willingness to stay awake. When you nurture your curiosity, you open yourself to growth, to connection, and to possibility. And that's not just personal—it's powerful.

## Final Roar

Curiosity is often the quiet spark that ignites extraordinary change. It's what drives us to take a second look, to open the next page, to question a pattern, or to wonder what else is possible. When we are curious, we remain open to learning, evolving, and expanding our understanding—not just of the world, but of ourselves.

In a world that often encourages us to stay in our lanes, follow the rules, or stick with what's familiar, choosing curiosity is a radical act of empowerment. It says: *I care enough to explore. I believe there's more out there—and more within me.*

Let that spark stay lit. Ask questions. Seek joy. Follow the breadcrumbs. You don't need to know exactly where the path leads—your curiosity will walk with you the whole way.

> *I am a curious soul, open to the wonder*
> *of learning, growth, and possibility.*
> *My questions lead me forward.*

# Insightful

## What It Means to Be Insightful

The Latin root of insightful comes from *insightus*, meaning "a sight into"—not just seeing with your eyes, but seeing into the heart of something. Insight doesn't always arrive like a lightning bolt. More often, it whispers. It nudges. It shows up in stillness and asks us to pause, reflect, and look again.

But here's the thing: Sometimes, we can't look clearly on our own. Sometimes, the most powerful insight comes when we dare to ask someone else to help us see what we cannot yet see ourselves.

I used to think being insightful meant being intuitive, emotionally intelligent, or quick to connect the dots. And sure, sometimes it does. But the most profound insights of my life didn't come through journaling, meditating or sitting in stillness. They came through therapy—hard, messy, vulnerable therapy.

And as a strong, independent woman, that was a really, really hard realization for me to accept. I mean, *really* hard. But that mirror—held up by someone else—was the only way I could truly see what needed to change. That insight didn't come from inside me. It came from being brave enough to let someone *show* me.

Let me give you some background.

I've had three long-term relationships in my life, each lasting nearly a decade. And after the third one ended, I knew something had to change. I couldn't keep replaying the same movie with different actors. But I didn't know what the pattern was. I couldn't see it. That was the most frustrating part—because I *felt* like I was doing the right things. I was caring. Supportive. Encouraging.

But therapy helped me see the truth I was avoiding: I wasn't just supporting my partners—I was *carrying* them. I had taken on the emotional weight of their dreams, their direction, and their drive. I was trying to hold everything together—again.

There was love—but that love eventually had twisted into over-functioning. I couldn't see where support ended and self-sacrifice began. What I thought was strength was control. And what I thought was generosity had quietly morphed into martyrdom.

That insight wrecked me—and then it freed me. Because once I saw the pattern, I could no longer deny it. And I knew something had to change.

Maybe you've experienced something similar. Perhaps you've found yourself wondering, *Why does this keep happening? How did I end up here again?* Insight isn't just about recognizing patterns. It's about being willing to face them. And sometimes, you can't do that alone. Sometimes, being insightful means being brave enough to say, *I need help seeing myself clearly.*

That's not weakness.

That's wisdom.

That's courage.

That's strength.

That personal act of admitting I couldn't do it alone, and letting someone help me see myself in the mirror—that changed everything for me. As I began to trust my own insight more, I also started noticing things I might've missed before. Years ago, I was in a meeting with a colleague who was usually upbeat—but that day, he seemed off. Something in me noticed the shift. After the meeting, I gently asked if everything was okay. He paused, then broke down. He and his wife were struggling to keep their business afloat. The pressure of being the provider, the fear of losing everything—they were weighing on him.

That moment reminded me that insight isn't just about perception—it's about connection. It's about noticing what's beneath the surface and responding with compassion and empathy. The more honest I became with myself, the more attuned I became to others.

In leadership, insight is a superpower. It allows you to read a room, anticipate tension, and name what others are too afraid to say. But the most crucial insight will always be the kind that helps you grow into a wiser, more self-aware version of yourself.

And sometimes, the wisest thing you can say is, *I can't see this clearly on my own.*

## Are You Holding Yourself Back?

Insight doesn't always come wrapped in clarity. Sometimes it comes wrapped in discomfort—quiet gut feelings, emotional weight, subtle shifts that you can't explain, but can't ignore.

The truth is, many of us sense more than we realize. We see the tension in the room. We feel when something's off. We recognize patterns long before others do. But instead of trusting that inner knowing, we often question it. We dismiss it. We ask for data instead of listening to our own depth.

Why? Because for so long, we've been taught to second-guess ourselves. To believe that instinct isn't valid unless it comes with proof.

*But what if your insight is the proof?*

You may be holding yourself back if:

- You've been told you "read too much into things," even when your gut told you something was off.
- You hesitate to speak up in meetings or conversations unless you can back your observation with data.
- You've had your insight reworded or repeated by someone else—only then to see it taken seriously.
- You downplay your intuition, assuming it's not as credible as logic or analytics.
- You recognize patterns but hold back from sharing them for fear of being labeled "too sensitive" or "too much."

If any of these sound familiar, it's time to *reclaim* your inner wisdom.

You don't need permission to notice what others miss. You don't need validation to speak what you feel. Being insightful doesn't mean you're dramatic—it means you're dialed in. Present. Awake. And brave enough to tell the truth that others aren't ready to say.

> *Insight is not something to shrink from.*
> *It's something to stand in.*

## Building the Skill: Strategies to Deepen Your Insight

Insight doesn't come by chance. It's cultivated—built piece by piece through reflection, emotional honesty, and the courage to ask hard questions. With each effort, your insight becomes clearer and more powerful.

Deepening your insight isn't just about self-awareness—it's about becoming the kind of woman who leads with clarity, lives with alignment, and loves with discernment.

Here are intentional ways to strengthen your insight and tune in more deeply to what matters:

1. **Practice active reflection.**
   Make space—daily or weekly—to ask yourself: *What just happened?* and *Why did it matter?* Go beyond surface analysis. Reflect on emotional impact, patterns, and internal cues. Write it out. Speak it aloud. Let the insight come through the pause.

2. **Pause before reacting.**
   Insightful people aren't impulsive—they're intentional. In emotionally charged moments, take a breath. Ask, *What else might be going on here?* That single pause can reveal the layer beneath the noise.

3. **Seek understanding, not just information.**
   When someone shares with you, go deeper. Ask: "What do you think this means for you?" or "What are you not saying yet?" These questions build a connection—and uncover powerful truths.

4. **Read between the lines.**

   Insight often lives in tone, timing, and tension. Pay attention to what's *not* being said. In emails, meetings, or body language—look for the gap between message and meaning.

5. **Trust your intuition.**

   If something feels "off" or "right," don't rush to override it with logic. Intuition is not the opposite of reason—it's a different kind of knowing. Honor it. Test it. Strengthen it.

6. **Share your perspective.**

   Don't keep your insight locked inside. Speak it with clarity and care. When you share what you see, you offer others the chance to shift, grow, or understand something they hadn't seen yet.

Insight grows in the spaces we create for it. When you give yourself room to reflect, connect, and listen deeply—both to yourself and to others—you don't just become more insightful. You become more grounded. More present. More powerful.

## Final Roar

Insight is more than knowledge—it is wisdom in motion. It's the ability to see the layers beneath the surface and respond with clarity, empathy, and truth.

Sometimes that truth comes from within. Other times, it comes through the mirror someone else holds up for you. Both require courage. Both require trust. And both are signs of strength.

When you honor your own inner knowing—and permit yourself to ask the hard questions, face the patterns, and speak what others won't—you step into a deeper kind of leadership.

*I am insightful.*
*I trust my inner wisdom*
*and see the deeper truth*
*with clarity, courage, and compassion.*

# Empathetic

## What It Means to Be Empathetic

Empathy is an intensely emotional and natural part of who I am. I'm not talking about textbook definitions or leadership buzzwords—I mean the kind of empathy that lives in your body. The kind that knocks the wind out of you when someone else is hurting. The kind that makes you feel a stranger's grief as if it were your own. The kind that makes you cry when someone else cries, even if you don't know why.

The word empathy comes from the Greek *empatheia*, meaning "passion or state of emotion," which stems from *en* (in) and *pathos* (feeling). To be empathetic means to "feel into" another person's emotional experience. But let's be clear—empathy is more than feeling *for* someone; it's about truly feeling *with* them.

Empathy also requires the courage to set aside your own beliefs and emotions—even for a moment—to imagine what someone else is experiencing. It's an imaginative act. That's why empathy is often misunderstood or confused with being "emotional." But they are not the same. Empathy is not weakness. It's strength, vulnerability, and connection all rolled into one.

I am what many would call a deep empath. I feel things intensely. It's more than compassion or kindness. It's a full-body, full-heart response to another person's reality.

There's also a common stereotype that women are more empathetic than men. Maybe we're socialized to recognize and respond to emotions differently, but I believe men are equally capable of empathy. In fact, in leadership roles—regardless of gender—empathy is essential. It's what allows you to see beyond numbers and performance and recognize the human being behind the role.

I want to share a time in my life that shaped my understanding of empathy in ways I'll never forget. I described this experience in a previous chapter, but here's a snapshot summary. I was going through a devastating breakup with someone I had been with for ten years. During that relationship, I had essentially raised his daughter from birth. She wasn't my biological child, but she was my daughter in every way that mattered.

Then, everything shattered. Without warning, he moved on with someone else, taking his daughter—*my daughter*—with him. I wasn't just grieving a breakup—I was mourning the loss of a child, of a family, of a future I had poured myself into. The pain was unimaginable. It truly felt like death.

In the aftermath, I was coasting through life on autopilot for almost a year. I went to work, but I wasn't there. I was a shell of myself. And yet, my manager at the time—someone I deeply respect—noticed. She didn't demand explanations or force me to perform at full capacity. Instead, she asked me gently if I wanted to talk. She made space. She gave me grace. She quietly asked others to pick up the slack where needed, and she never once made me feel ashamed or inadequate.

Her empathy didn't just help me survive that season—it taught me how to lead. Because when you've been held with compassion, you carry that forward. You learn to notice what others might miss. You understand that presence is sometimes more potent than performance. And you begin to lead not just with strategy, but with soul.

And it wasn't just her. Two dear friends also saw me during that time— really saw me. They recognized the weight I was carrying and knew I couldn't bear it alone. After work, on weekends, for months, they took me under their wings. We ate, talked, laughed, and cried. They never tried to fix it. They just sat with me in my sorrow, so I didn't have to face the silence of that empty house alone. Their empathy carried me through the hours in between—and I will never forget it.

To those two dear friends—

We may not talk every day now, but your impact on my life will never be forgotten. You helped me survive. You carried me when I couldn't walk on my own. Thank you for loving me through the darkest season with such quiet, unwavering empathy. I will always be grateful.

That's what empathy in leadership looks like—it's quiet, human, and incredibly powerful.

It's recognizing the humanity of every person who works with and for you. It's understanding that not everyone can flip the switch on and off like a light when transitioning from home to work and back again. Sometimes, work and life blend into a messy blob of chaos. It's in those moments, as leaders, that we all have an opportunity to be *better humans.* That is when we have the chance to *shine as leaders*—and to *show up* for our people in ways they may not otherwise expect. My manager did that for me, and I hope that all of us can follow her lead.

## Are You Holding Yourself Back?

Empathy is one of the most powerful forms of connection we have—but many of us were taught to keep it locked away.

Maybe you were told to "toughen up," to "leave it at the door," or to stop getting so emotionally involved. Perhaps you learned that being empathetic made you seem weak, dramatic, or too soft to be a leader. Over time, those messages can chip away at your natural instinct to care—and convince you that empathy has no place in strong decision-making.

But here's the truth: real leadership doesn't require emotional distance. It requires emotional depth.

And sometimes, we suppress empathy not because we don't care—but because *we're the ones hurting.* When you're burned out, emotionally raw, or running on fumes, it can feel impossible to show up for someone else. That's okay. You can't pour from an empty cup. But when you allow yourself to care deeply and respond sincerely, empathy becomes one of your greatest strengths.

Take a moment and ask yourself:

- Do I allow myself to feel what others feel, or do I instinctively try to "fix" or "solve" it?
- Am I afraid that showing empathy will make me vulnerable?
- Do I offer empathy to others more easily than I offer it to myself?

Don't rush through these questions. Sit with them. Let them uncover what's been buried or silenced. Insight begins in reflection. And empathy begins with you.

*The more you honor your own emotions,*
*the more space you create*
*to hold others*
*with care, strength, and humanity.*

## Building the Skill: Practicing Empathy

Even if empathy comes naturally to you, it's still a skill that must be nurtured and protected. And if it doesn't come easily? Don't worry—empathy can be strengthened into a powerful mindset.

Empathy requires presence. It asks you to slow down, open your heart, and meet people where they are—not where you expect them to be. And it requires care—not just for others, but for yourself. Because when you're the one others lean on, your emotional well-being matters, too.

Here are five ways to practice and protect your empathy:

1. **Listen to understand, not to respond.**
   Empathy starts with listening—authentic, open-hearted listening. That means quieting the urge to fix or reply, and simply being with someone in their moment. Listen for the emotion beneath the words. Listen for what's not being said.
2. **Ask, "What might they be feeling?"**

When someone shares something with you, pause before reacting. Ask yourself, *If I were in their shoes, how would I feel?* That single question can change your entire response.

3. **Practice empathetic curiosity.**

Don't assume you understand someone's experience—ask with genuine care. "Can you tell me more about that?" or "What was that like for you?" Questions like these open doors to connection.

4. **Hold space without trying to fix.**

Sometimes the most loving thing you can do is sit beside someone in silence. No silver linings. No solutions. Just presence. Your willingness to *be there* without changing anything is powerful.

5. **Tend to your own emotional health.**

If you're a natural empath, protect your energy. You can't absorb everyone's pain and keep going without replenishment. Boundaries are not the opposite of empathy—they are what enables empathy to survive.

Empathy isn't about carrying the weight of the world—it's about showing up with heart, even when it's hard. It's a daily choice to remain open and human in a world that often rewards distance and detachment.

And here's the hard truth: *a lack of empathy can do real damage*. When someone is unraveling—personally, emotionally, spiritually—and their pain is met with criticism or cold indifference, it can break them. Not just at work. In life. A harsh word, a dismissive look, a refusal to see someone's humanity in their hardest moment...

For someone barely holding it together, *that kind of indifference can be the final blow that shatters them.*

As leaders, friends, partners, and people—we hold the power to either deplete someone or help them keep it together. Your empathy might be the one thing that allows someone to rise instead of falling apart.

Whether you're leading a team or comforting a friend, never underestimate the power of your presence.

And if you are the one unraveling or feeling depleted right now, know that you are not alone. *I see you. I care about you.* There is help, hope, and healing available. Please take a moment to explore the *You Are Not Alone* section at the back of this book for resources and support.

## Final Roar

Empathy is not weakness. It is one of the fiercest forms of strength.
To feel what others feel,
to stand beside them in their sorrow or joy,
to hold space without fixing, solving, or turning away—
that takes courage—not fragility.

In a world that often tells us to numb out, toughen up, or "leave it at the door," choosing empathy is a rebellious act of leadership. It's a refusal to disconnect. It's how we build trust, how we lead with humanity, and how we change lives.

# Thoughtful

## What It Means to Be Thoughtful

The word thoughtful often gets watered down—reduced to polite gestures or small niceties. But genuine thoughtfulness runs much deeper. It's not just about remembering birthdays or saying thank you. It's about emotional presence. It's about choosing to notice what others overlook—and acting on that awareness.

Think about a time when someone saw you. Really saw you. When they reached out—not because they had to, but because they sensed something. That's the kind of thoughtfulness I'm talking about.

For me, being thoughtful means paying attention. It means slowing down enough to notice when someone's energy shifts. When they're quieter than usual. When their camera is off, three meetings in a row. When they say they're "fine"—but you can tell they're not.

I've learned over the years that the most thoughtful people aren't always the ones who bring the cupcakes or write the perfect note. They're the ones who stay emotionally tuned in. Who remember what matters to others. Who follow up. Who take the time to pause and ask, "Are you okay?"—even when it would be easier just to move on.

It might be a message that says, "Thinking of you today."

It might be a compliment that feels strangely well-timed.

It might be simply staying quiet and present when someone needs space to process.

These aren't grand gestures. They're intentional choices to lead with care. And they mean something. They remind people that they matter, that they're seen, and that they're not alone in whatever they're carrying.

Even something as simple as "How are you?" can be powerful—if you mean it. Too often, it's become a throwaway phrase, something we ask without really wanting the answer. But when you ask it with intention, and when you're willing to truly listen to the response, that question becomes an invitation.

"How are you... really?"

That's where thoughtfulness begins. In creating the kind of space where people feel safe enough to answer honestly.

Some of the most thoughtful people I've known were going through their own silent struggles behind the scenes. But they still showed up for others—not because they had it all together, but because they understood how powerful it is to feel noticed.

That's what real thoughtfulness is. It's not performative. It's relational. It's not about being liked—it's about being present.

When I was recovering from breast cancer surgery, my coworkers did something that still brings me to tears when I think about it. Every Friday, they dressed in pink and stood together to form the shape of a breast cancer ribbon. Then they'd snap a photo—smiling, arms linked, united in support—and send it to me.

Week after week, those photos showed up on my phone like little bursts of sunshine. They didn't just lift my spirits—they reminded me that I was still part of something bigger, still connected, still held. I wasn't forgotten. I wasn't alone. That's the kind of thoughtfulness that doesn't just brighten a moment—it carries you through it.

I once worked with a woman who had a gift for that heartfelt, genuine thoughtfulness. She wasn't loud or flashy in the traditional sense, but she showed up in life with class and flare—from her high-heeled colorful shoes to her glamorous smile. She wore her heart on her sleeve in the most authentic way. And what made her unforgettable wasn't just her style—it was how she showed up for people. She remembered people's names. Their kids' names.

Their birthdays, their favorite hobbies, even which days someone had a hard meeting. It wasn't about collecting details—it was about honoring people. She didn't lead with dominance—she led with presence.

And watching her taught me something that's stayed with me to this day: Thoughtfulness is a form of leadership. Quiet. Intentional. Lasting.

Watching her taught me that being thoughtful isn't about perfection—it's about presence. And you don't have to be in charge to lead with thoughtfulness. You just have to care enough to notice—and act.

## Are You Holding Yourself Back?

Sometimes, being thoughtful gets a bad reputation.

We're told not to "overthink," not to "be so sensitive," or not to "worry too much about other people." Thoughtfulness is often mistaken for fragility, especially in high-pressure environments that reward speed over depth.

But the truth is that thoughtfulness is not a sign of weakness. It's leadership. It's emotional intelligence in motion.

In today's world, where productivity often gets more praise than presence, thoughtfulness can feel like a rebellious act. But when we choose to slow down, notice, and respond with care, we aren't falling behind—we're moving through the world with intention. And that changes everything.

Every check-in, every moment of pause, every time we choose people over pressure—we're creating space for something deeper: trust, connection, belonging.

Consider these questions:

- Are you holding back your natural thoughtfulness because you're afraid it will be seen as soft or inefficient?
- Are you pushing past emotional cues—your own or someone else's— because you don't think you have the time to slow down?
- Have you ever wanted to check on someone, offer support, or acknowledge a moment... and then talked yourself out of it?
- Do you ever assume someone else will say something kind, so you stay

quiet—even when you feel the nudge to speak up?

- Have you trained yourself to "keep it moving," even when your heart is whispering, *Pause. Pay attention. This matters?*

If so, you're not alone. And it's not too late to shift.

Genuine thoughtfulness doesn't require a perfect script or a formal role. It starts with awareness. With care. Being willing to stop—just for a moment—and *really see* someone.

When you practice thoughtful presence, you make space for connection. You give people permission to feel. And you model a different kind of strength—the kind that leads not with force, but with humanity.

## Building the Skill: How to Practice Thoughtfulness

Thoughtfulness is not about being perfect or polished. It's about being present.

You don't need the right words. You don't need a detailed plan. You just need to be willing to show up—with your full attention and a little courage.

Here are a few ways to practice thoughtful leadership in everyday life:

1. **Pause before responding.**
   If someone shares something vulnerable, resist the urge to immediately solve or redirect. Give it space. Let the moment breathe.
2. **Notice the details.**
   If a colleague seems off, if a friend becomes quiet, or if your child hesitates—ask a gentle question. Thoughtfulness lives in noticing what others rush past.
3. **Follow up.**
   Thoughtfulness doesn't end with one check-in. If someone shares a struggle with you, follow up later. "Hey, I've been thinking about you—how are things going?" Those small reminders can mean everything.
4. **Offer specific support.**
   Instead of "Let me know if you need anything," try "I'd love to drop

off dinner this week—would Wednesday or Thursday work better?"
That kind of thoughtfulness removes pressure and makes it easier for
someone to receive care.

5. **Acknowledge the invisible load.**

   Many people carry burdens you'll never see. A simple, "I know you're
   doing a lot, and I just want to say I notice and appreciate you," can be
   incredibly affirming.

6. **Extend grace.**

   We never know what someone's battling behind the scenes. When in
   doubt, choose kindness. Choose patience. Choose the benefit of the
   doubt.

Being thoughtful doesn't mean over-functioning or people-pleasing. It
means honoring your own emotional intelligence—and using it to lift,
support, and lead with empathy.

## Final Roar

Thoughtfulness doesn't always look like strength from the outside.
But it is.
It's the courage to show up when it's awkward,
to speak when it's quiet,
to notice when others look away.

It's the quiet leadership that reminds others:
you matter, you're seen, you're not alone.

It's a way of being that makes the world
a gentler, kinder, and more connected place.
In a world that often feels rushed, distracted, and divided,
thoughtfulness—and the willingness to care—
are quiet but radical forms of leadership.

I notice.

I care.

I act with presence and compassion.

My thoughtfulness is not a weakness.

It is a strength.

And I lead with it, boldly.

*The world doesn't need louder voices.*
*It needs deeper presence.*
*Let your thoughtfulness*
*be the quiet roar*
*that changes everything.*

# Inspirational

## What It Means to Be Inspirational

The word inspirational traces back to the Latin verb *inspirare*—"to breathe into." That's what inspiration does. It fills us with energy, with hope, with the courage to take one more step, even when we're not sure where it will lead.

Think about a time when someone inspired you—not because they were famous, or flawless, or loud, but because they moved you. Because they made you believe in something bigger. Because they reminded you of your own power.

When I think of inspirational leaders, I think of Amanda Gorman—who stood on the Capitol steps at just 22 and used poetry to speak hope into a divided nation. I think of Brené Brown, whose research and vulnerability have helped millions of people lead with more courage and heart. And I think of the women we don't see in headlines—caregivers, mentors, community builders—who keep showing up, not because the world is watching, but because it matters.

Inspiration isn't something loud or performative. It's something *felt*. It lives in persistence. In presence. In the quiet strength of someone who chooses to act with purpose, even when no one's paying attention.

And often, we don't even realize when we're being inspirational to someone else.

You might not feel brave. You might feel like you're barely holding it together. But someone, somewhere, sees how you keep going—and thinks: *If she can do it, maybe I can too.*

That's how I learned that being inspirational doesn't mean having it all together—it means living in a way that breathes courage into someone else.

I once worked with a woman who had just joined our team. She was new to the organization, soft-spoken, and still finding her footing. During a team meeting, a more senior male colleague interrupted her mid-sentence—twice. I could see her shrink. Her voice faltered. She gave up on finishing her thought.

I felt that moment deeply because I've been there too—talked over, overlooked, dismissed.

So I spoke up.

I interrupted *him* and redirected attention back to her. I said, "I think she was in the middle of a point—can we give her space to finish?" It wasn't rehearsed or dramatic. It was a moment of presence and protection. After the meeting, she pulled me aside and said, "Thank you. You didn't just give me space—you gave me permission to keep speaking up."

That's what inspiration looks like. It's not a viral moment or a highlight reel. It's one person making space for another. One decision to use your voice in service of someone else's.

I didn't fix anything in that moment. But I shifted something. I sent a signal that said, *You belong here. Your voice matters.* And in doing that, I reminded myself of the quiet power we all carry—to redirect attention, to reinforce respect, to challenge the tone in a room with calm, intentional presence.

But that moment wasn't just for her.

It was also for the person who interrupted her. It was a disruption of behavior he may not have even realized had impact. A mirror held up—not with blame, but with accountability. That small act may have prompted him to engage in his own self-reflection. And maybe next time, he'll catch himself. Maybe next time, he'll do better. Perhaps he'll even be the one who makes space for someone else.

Inspiration isn't always loud. Sometimes, it tiptoes quietly through the room and starts a ripple no one can see right away. That's the kind of inspiration I want to live out—not performative, but powerful.

> *It's not about being the star of the show,*
> *but about igniting the fire in others—*
> *that's the legacy of a lioness roar.*

We all have that power.

You don't have to change the world to be inspirational.

You just have to live your truth—and be willing to stand beside someone else as they find theirs.

## Are You Holding Yourself Back?

You may not even realize the impact you can have on others.

So often, we associate the word inspirational with public figures, polished speeches, or dramatic life transformations—and we forget that inspiration happens in the everyday moments. Through kindness. Through honesty. Through resilience and presence.

But if you're constantly second-guessing your worth or staying silent out of fear, you may be holding back the very spark someone else needs to see.

You don't have to be famous to make an impact. You don't need a platform to change someone's perspective. You just need to be willing to live your truth—out loud.

Take a moment to reflect:

- Do you believe you have to be wildly successful or overcome something dramatic to inspire others?
- Are you downplaying your story because you think it's "not big enough" or "not impressive enough" to matter?
- Do you hesitate to share your truth for fear of being seen as vulnerable or attention-seeking?
- Have you dismissed compliments from others about how you've inspired

them because it feels uncomfortable to own that impact?

· Are you waiting for the "perfect time" to speak up, step up, or show up in your authentic power?

If you nodded yes to any of these—know this: you're not alone.

But also know: someone is always watching. Someone is always listening. And your small act of bravery, kindness, or truth-telling could be the spark they need.

You don't have to feel inspirational to *be* inspirational.

You just have to be willing to act with purpose—even when it's uncomfortable.

## Building the Skill: Inspiring with Grace and Genuine Presence

Inspiration isn't about being impressive. It's about being real.

We don't need more perfection—we need more presence. We need more women showing up fully as themselves, unfiltered and honest, especially in a world that still tries to mute and mold us.

Here are a few ways to lead with lioness-inspired fire and finesse:

1. **Live in alignment.**
   When your actions reflect your values, you naturally inspire others. Integrity leaves a trail.

2. **Own your story.**
   Share the hard parts, not just the polished ones. People don't connect with perfection—they connect with truth.

3. **Stand for something.**
   Whether it's a belief, a boundary, or a cause—let people know what you care about and why.

4. **Let your scars speak.**
   If you've walked through fire and made it to the other side, you have wisdom that someone else is praying for.

5. **Use your voice.**
   Speak up, even when it's hard. Especially when it's hard. You never know who's watching and learning from your example.

6. **Celebrate others.**
   One of the most inspirational things you can do is shine light on someone else's growth and grit.

7. **Stay grounded.**
   You don't have to be the loudest in the room. Often, it's your steadiness that people admire most.

Remember, inspiration isn't something you chase. It's something you embody.

## Final Roar

You don't have to be the boldest, the strongest, or the most accomplished to inspire others. You just have to be *you*.

Fully. Authentically. Imperfectly.

The way you rise after falling. The way you love through loss. The way you speak with conviction, even when your voice shakes—that's what moves people.

The most powerful kind of inspiration comes from living your life with purpose and refusing to shrink.

*So stop waiting for permission.*
*Speak up.*
*Show up.*
*Tell the truth.*
*Shine anyway.*

Let your presence light the path.

Let your leadership lift others.

Let your life be a whisper, a shout, a spark—

whatever it needs to be to remind someone else:

*You've got this, too.*

**Let this be your Inspirational Roar:**

*I am a force of light, grounded in truth and ignited by purpose.*

*I don't wait to be inspirational—I choose to be it, every single day.*

*My story matters. My voice echoes.*

*I lead with heart, I rise with vision, and I lift with love.*

*I am not just inspired.*

*I am inspirational.*

*And I will never dim my roar again.*

# Motivational

## What It Means to Be Motivational

The Latin root of the word motivate is *movere*, meaning "to move." And isn't that precisely what a motivational person does? They stir something within you. They light a spark. They get you to move—toward a dream, a goal, or simply to take the next brave step.

For me, being motivational isn't about delivering speeches or quoting clichés—it's about living in a way that compels others to believe in possibility. And that belief has to start with me. With my story. With the hardest parts of my life, where I had to find a way to move forward before I ever encouraged anyone else to do the same.

During my breast cancer journey, I was fortunate in many ways. My treatment didn't involve chemotherapy or radiation. Instead, I chose what my doctors considered a radical route: a double mastectomy with reconstruction. I didn't lose my hair. I didn't bear the burns of radiation. But I did have to stand in front of the mirror and embrace the scars from multiple surgeries—every single day.

And let me be honest: I didn't immediately embrace them.

There were days I collapsed on the bathroom floor, sobbing, because of how much I hated those scars. Because I never asked for cancer. I never wanted this. I felt disfigured. Betrayed by my body. I was still in denial, still clinging to the version of myself that didn't carry those wounds. There were years—yes, years—of emotional whiplash, riding a roller coaster between self-love and self-loathing.

It took time. And therapy. And grace. And deep, private work. But eventually, I made it through.

Today, I look at those scars and I don't see shame. I see strength. I see fire. I see undeniable proof that I chose life. That I chose healing. That I chose *me*.

Those scars tell a story—not of what broke me, but of what I was willing to fight for.

Not of what I lost, but of how fiercely I showed up to reclaim my power.

I now wear those scars as a badge of honor—a visible, living testament to my resilience. And as I embrace them, they remind me of something vital:

I can never allow my roar to be dimmed.

Because I've already fought too hard to find it.

Because there is power in survival—and even greater power in choosing to rise again.

Because my story, with all its pain and beauty, might be the very thing that gives another woman permission to rise, too.

That's what it means to be motivational. Not just to light a fire in someone else—but to learn how to spark one in *yourself*, even when the room is dark and silent and no one is cheering you on.

After my recovery, I began sharing my story publicly at speaking events. I used my experience to motivate women to get screened, because I was living proof that early detection saves lives. To this day, I still receive messages from women who tell me they went for their annual screening because of my story. That was the moment I realized: you don't need a stage to be motivational—you just need to be real.

I'll never forget one particular speaking engagement as a United Way Torchmaker, when I was asked to speak at a corporate event and share my story. I stood before a room filled with both men and women—some survivors, some caregivers, and some simply seeking answers. As I spoke, I could feel the weight of shared experience settle into the room. When I talked about looking in the mirror for the first time after surgery, one woman started to cry. Afterward, she pulled me aside and said, "I've been putting off my mammogram for years. My mom had breast cancer, and I've been too scared to move forward and get tested. But, I'm calling to schedule it tomorrow." That moment reminded me that motivation isn't always loud. Sometimes, it's a whisper that says: *If she can do it, maybe I can too.*

But my motivational moments haven't only come from stages or spotlights. They've come from late-night phone calls with friends, pep talks with team members who'd lost their spark, and quiet conversations where someone needed to borrow just a bit of belief from me until they could find their own again.

Because being motivational isn't about performance, it's about presence. It's about using your life—messy, complicated, real—as proof that progress is possible. That healing is possible. That motion is possible.

Motivation is not about perfection. It's about motion. And when your motion is purposeful, passionate, and persistent, it naturally pulls others forward with you.

## Are You Holding Yourself Back?

Not everyone sees themselves as motivational—and often, it's because we underestimate the quiet power of our own resilience. We think motivation has to be loud, flashy, or perfect. But it doesn't. Sometimes, the most motivational thing in the world is watching someone get back up after life knocks them flat.

You might think: *Who am I to inspire anyone?* But here's the truth: you don't motivate others by having it all together. You motivate them by being real. By being honest about the struggle. By choosing hope when it's hard, and motion when it's messy.

Sometimes the very thing you're most hesitant to share—that one moment of vulnerability you're terrified to let breathe—may be the exact story someone else needs to hear.

Motivation shows up in many forms. It's the colleague who quietly cheers you on during a tough week. It's the single mom who keeps showing up for her kids when she's running on fumes. It's the woman staring in the mirror, learning how to love herself again after everything she's lost.

That kind of motivation is powerful because it's real—and it's all around us.

Ask yourself:

- Do I downplay my story because I think it's not "inspiring enough"?
- Am I waiting for the perfect platform or perfect version of myself before I share what I've lived through?
- Do I hold back from encouraging others because I don't want to seem pushy—or afraid I'll sound like a cliché?
- Have I convinced myself that my voice doesn't matter?
- Do I shrink when others look to me for strength, wondering if I'm truly qualified to lead?

Let me remind you:

> *If you've ever gotten back up after falling,*
> *if you've ever chosen hope over despair,*
> *or if you've kept moving*
> *when you felt like giving up—*
> *you are already motivational.*

The question is: Are you willing to own it?

And if today you're still struggling—if standing up feels hard and motivation feels far away—that doesn't make you *less*. That makes you *human*. And if no one else tells you this today, hear it from me: I **care** about you, and I **believe** in you.

Let me be your voice right now. Let me say what you might not be ready to say to yourself:

*You are stronger than you think.*
*And your story—*
*yes, even the messy, unfinished parts—*
*has the power*
*to move someone else forward.*

## Building the Skill: How to Be More Motivational

Motivation isn't something you either have or don't have—it's something you build. Quietly. Daily. In private moments when no one's watching, and in public moments when someone else needs your strength.

You don't have to be on a stage to be motivational. You just have to live in motion—with honesty, purpose, and heart.

Here are some powerful ways to strengthen your ability to motivate not only yourself, but others:

1. **Share from your scars, not your wounds.**
   Let your healing—whether from illness, grief, heartbreak, or transition—become a source of power for others. Speak when you're ready, and when your story can lift with hope instead of awaken pain. Strength shared honestly becomes strength multiplied.

2. **Be transparent with your process.**
   People don't connect with perfection—they connect with progress. Share what you're learning in real time. Talk about the messy middle, not just the polished outcome. Motivation lives in relatability.

3. **Infuse your words with purpose.**
   Whether it's a text to a friend or a note to your team, speak with clarity and care. One sentence—spoken with intention—can shift someone's entire day.

4. **Practice motivational listening.**
   Sometimes, the most inspiring thing you can do is hold space. Really listen. Reflect back someone's strength. Say things like, "I see how hard you're trying," or "You're doing better than you think."

5. **Lead by example.**

When others see you showing up, pushing forward, honoring your values—even on the hard days—they'll believe they can too. You don't need a title. You need consistency.

6. **Create a ripple effect.**

Leave people better than you found them. Write the note. Give the compliment. Share the resource. Speak life into someone who's tired. You never know who needed that extra push to keep going.

7. **Celebrate others loudly and often.**

People rise when they feel seen. Be the one who names their effort. Notice their growth. Recognize their resilience. Your encouragement might be the spark they've been waiting for.

8. **Speak possibility.**

When someone is stuck in doubt, offer a shift in perspective—not false hope, but real belief in their strength. Say, "I believe in you," or "What if this is the beginning of something better?"

Being motivational isn't about performance. It's about alignment. When you live a life rooted in truth, fueled by purpose, and open to connection, your presence becomes its own kind of encouragement.

## Final Roar

You don't need a title to be motivational. You don't need a stage, a platform, or the perfect story. You just need motion. Forward, faithful, purpose-filled motion.

Even when you're tired. Even when the spotlight fades. Even when no one's clapping yet.

You may never know the full impact of your story, your words, or your quiet acts of courage. But someone out there is watching you rise—and believing they can too.

Motivation doesn't have to be loud. It doesn't have to be perfect. It just has to be true.

Keep showing up.

Keep choosing motion.

The world doesn't need another flawless highlight reel.

It needs more real, resilient women who lead with heart.

*I rise with purpose.*

*I speak with courage.*

*My life moves others forward—because I keep moving.*

**Let this be your roar.**

**Because women like us do not stop—**

**we rise, we roar, and we lead fiercely.**

**And this is only the beginning.**

# You Are Not Alone

If you or someone you love is struggling with mental health challenges, emotional distress, or thoughts of suicide, please know *you are not alone*—and you do not have to carry the weight by yourself. The following national resources provide confidential and compassionate support. Many are available 24 hours a day, 7 days a week.

## Immediate Crisis Support

### 988 Suicide & Crisis Lifeline
☎ Call or Text **988**
⊕ 988lifeline.org
Free and confidential support for people in emotional distress or suicidal crisis. Also available via online chat. *If you are in a crisis at any time, please call or text 988.*

### Crisis Text Line
▯ Text **HOME** or **HOLA** to **741741**
⊕ crisistextline.org
Text-based support from trained crisis counselors, available 24/7.

## Mental Health & Substance Use Support

**National Alliance on Mental Illness (NAMI)**

📞 NAMI HelpLine: **1-800-950-NAMI (6264)**

Text **helpline** to **62640**

🌐 nami.org/help

Offers peer support, education, and resource referrals Monday–Friday, 10 AM–10 PM ET.

**Substance Abuse and Mental Health Services Administration (SAMHSA)**

📞 National Helpline: **1-800-662-HELP (4357)**

📟 TTY Helpline: **1-800-487-4889**

🌐 samhsa.gov/find-help/national-helpline

Confidential help and referrals for mental health and substance use treatment.

## Specialized Support Services

**The Trevor Project** (*Support for LGBTQ+ Youth*)

📞 **1-866-488-7386**

📱 Text **START** to **678678**

🌐 thetrevorproject.org

Life-saving support for LGBTQ+ youth in crisis.

**Veterans Crisis Line**

📞 Dial **988**, then press **1**

📱 Text a message to **838255**

🌐 veteranscrisisline.net

24/7 support for veterans, service members, and their families.

**RAINN (Rape, Abuse & Incest National Network)**
📞 1-800-656-HOPE (4673)
🌐 rainn.org
Support for survivors of sexual assault and abuse.

**Trans Lifeline**
📞 1-877-565-8860 (US)
📞 1-877-330-6366 (Canada)
🌐 translifeline.org
Peer support and crisis line run by and for the transgender community.

*The resources listed here were accurate at the time of publication. Please check the official websites for the most current information, or contact local organizations in your area for additional support.* **Remember that you are not alone!**

# The First Roar

This book began with a whisper—a memory, a question, a quiet nudge in the dark. It began in the soft spaces we so often hide, in the places we've been told to be small.

But look how far you've come.

You've walked through pages that asked you to remember your voice. To challenge old patterns. To embrace your beauty, your power, your truth. You've met parts of yourself you may have buried long ago—and you've reminded them they're welcome here.

If you've made it to this page, it's because you were never meant to live a quiet life. You were meant to lead, to create, to disrupt, to heal. You were meant to ROAR.

So keep going. Roar in the boardroom. Roar in your relationships. Roar when it's uncomfortable. Roar when it's joyful. Roar when it changes everything.

And when the world tries to hand you silence, hand it your voice instead.

You don't need permission. You don't need perfection. You just need truth, intention, and the courage to show up as yourself—again and again.

This isn't the end of your story.

And it's definitely not the end of mine.

This is **only the first roar.**

*I am not here to take up less space.*
*And neither are you.*
—Ronda K. Salazar

**Act on everything #WithPurpose.**

235

# About the Author

**Ronda K. Salazar** is a writer, empowerment advocate, and breast cancer survivor who believes in the power of purpose, presence, and persistence. After years of navigating corporate leadership, creative side hustles, and life's biggest challenges, she found her voice—and her roar—by choosing to live *#WithPurpose*.

Through her writing, music, and mentorship, Ronda helps others rediscover their worth, reclaim their power, and rise with clarity and courage. She is the founder of *Act With Purpose Publishing* and the heartbeat behind the *Roar Like A Woman* movement —challenging women to rise up, embrace their inner lioness, and keep roaring.

She lives boldly, loves fiercely, and leads with purpose—every single day.

# Connect with Ronda

This book may be coming to an end, but your roar is just getting started.

I'd love to hear how *Roar Like A Woman* inspired you—your reflections, your favorite word, or your own story of reclaiming your voice.

You can connect with me, share your story, and access new tools and resources by visiting:

**www.RoarLikeAWomanOfficial.com**

Email: **Ronda@RoarLikeAWomanOfficial.com**

As the *Roar Like A Woman* movement grows, you'll find updates on companion journals, upcoming events, and more ways to keep showing up, keep shining, and keep roaring.

Follow the hashtag *#RoarLikeAWoman* to join the conversation.

Your voice matters.

Your fire matters.

And your roar? The world needs it now more than ever.

*#KeepRoaring*